MASTERING
THE PASTORAL
ROLE

MASTERING
THE PASTORAL ROLE

Paul Cedar
Kent Hughes
Ben Patterson

MULTNOMAH

Portland, Oregon 97266

Christianity Today, Inc.

MASTERING THE PASTORAL ROLE
© 1991 by Christianity Today, Inc.
Published by Multnomah Press
10209 SE Division Street
Portland, Oregon 97266

Multnomah Press is a ministry of Multnomah School of the Bible, 8435 NE Glisan Street, Portland, Oregon 97220.

Printed in the United States of America.

Library of Congress Cataloging-in-Publication Data

Cedar, Paul A., 1938-
    Mastering the pastoral role / Paul Cedar, Kent Hughes, Ben Patterson.
       p. cm. — (Mastering ministry)
    ISBN 0-88070-439-X
    1. Pastoral theology—United States. 2. Clergy—United States—Office. I. Hughes, R. Kent. II. Patterson, Ben, 1942-III. Title. IV. Series.
BV4011.C39   1991
253—dc20   91-8436
                                                CIP

91 92 93 94 95 96 97 98 99 00 - 10 9 8 7 6 5 4 3 2 1

Contents

Introduction

I'd been on staff at Millbrook Presbyterian for a couple of weeks when Pastor Bradley told me to get a haircut. He wasn't that blunt, but I got the message. He also said, tactfully again, that I ought to dress better. Apparently he meant it: he offered to lend me money to buy some new clothes.

I was not pleased. Yes, it was a suburban church, but I was minister to youth, not readers of *GQ*. All right, I wore a longish, early 1970s shag. Okay, my jeans were a little faded, maybe torn here or there. But my tee shirts were pretty new.

I fumed when I got home, but my wife, and seemingly everyone else in the galaxy, understood that those entering ministry have to give up some of their freedom. I thought the entire galaxy stupid, but I went along.

By the time I left pastoral ministry, I regularly wore a coat and tie, sometimes even a clerical collar, and I didn't even flinch. I'd gotten used to the idea that the pastorate is more than being yourself; the pastor also has a role to fulfill.

The Pastoral Balancing Act

Just because I'd gotten used to the idea did not mean I knew exactly when and how to play that role. The further out I walked on the tightrope of ministry, the more difficult it was to maintain my balance:

On the one hand, pastors are supposed to lead and challenge people, with visionary preaching and careful administration, into uncharted wildernesses to discover new promised lands, flowing with milk and honey. On the other hand, we should be tender shepherds, accepting people where they are, as they are, carefully loving them.

On the one hand, pastors, as people of God, should throw themselves sacrificially into their work and strive relentlessly for excellence in all they do, never shirking any task or person who needs ministerial attention. On the other hand, we are supposed to guard jealously our family and personal time.

On the one hand, pastors should respond to "the call," going eagerly, rapidly, wherever God designates, no matter the pay, no matter the difficulty of the mission. On the other hand, some calls wreak havoc with a dossier and make getting another call nearly impossible; we can't feed our families like that.

And on it goes. Pastors are asked to be Winston Churchill and Mother Theresa, Joan of Arc and Ward Cleaver. It can give one a headache.

It's not easy balancing our pastoral and personal selves as well as our roles as seer and servant. But I dare say you do it all the time — otherwise, you wouldn't have a job or your sanity. Still, most pastors admit to needing to do it better.

So for this volume of Mastering Ministry we've brought together three authors who not only know the headaches that fulfilling the pastoral role brings but who also know how to spell *relief*.

Paul Cedar

When Paul Cedar began pastoral ministry at a small Evangelical Free Church in Naperville, Illinois, there were only nineteen people in essentially three families in the church. Driving from Denver with his wife, Jeannie, and two sons (their daughter had yet to be born), he pondered what he was going to do when he arrived.

He finally said to his wife, "Honey, I don't know what I'm going to do the second day. I know what I'm going to do the first day. The first day I'm going to visit all three families; I'm going to talk with them and get to know them. But what am I going to do the second day?"

Well, he's never laid his head on his pillow at night wondering what he's going to do the next day. And all through his ministry, he has combined conscientiousness with administrative efficiency with pastoral concern.

After Naperville, Paul became crusade director for the Leighton Ford evangelistic team. After that he served three churches in California: as senior pastor of Evangelical Free Church of Yorba Linda, executive pastor of Hollywood Presbyterian Church in Hollywood, and senior pastor of Lake Avenue Congregational in Pasadena.

Paul brings to this volume not only a varied experience in the pastorate, but a vicarious experience of working with hundreds of other pastors whom he now serves: since 1990 he's been president of the Evangelical Church of America, headquarted in Minneapolis, Minnesota.

In addition, he's written *The Communicator's Commentary: James, 1, 2 Peter, Jude* (Word) and *Strength in Servant Leadership* (Word).

Kent Hughes

Most pastors hang on their office walls mementos and Christian symbols, and perhaps a degree or two. I'm sure Kent Hughes has such things to hang, but I never noticed, for his office is lined (this is no metaphor) with books.

You'd never suspect his acquaintance with books, though, when you make his acquaintance, because he shows a focused interest in the person he's talking to. On top of that, add accomplished preaching and effective administration, and you soon recognize that Kent is one of a dying breed, a pastoral generalist, one who does a lot of things well.

He's nurtured his varied skills through two pastorates in California, one a church plant. Since 1979 he has been senior pastor of College Church in Wheaton, Illinois.

Kent also has written many books, among others: commentaries on Colossians, Mark, and Ephesians in the Preaching the Word series (Crossway) and, with his wife, Barbara, *Liberating Ministry from the Success Syndrome* (Tyndale).

Ben Patterson

You can take the boy out of Southern California, but you can't take Southern California out of the boy.

I suppose that's why Ben Patterson still sports a beard and wears an open collar and sweater to the office — even though he's pastor of New Providence Presbyterian Church, a tall, white church with a steeple atop, graveyard around, and a colonial sanctuary (with doors to each pew) within; located in a New Jersey town of the same name, a small, woodsy Eastern community from which many commute to Wall Street or the headquarters of IBM or AT&T.

And you can put Ben Patterson in genteel and proper surroundings, but you're still going to get a man who is direct, earthy, brash, an iconoclast. At the same time, he can be disarming in his willingness to acknowledge his faults. But what comes across most is his passion to minister.

He's brought that passion to a number of settings, all previously in California. He was an associate pastor at La Jolla Presbyterian Church for four years and founding pastor of Irvine Presbyterian Church, where he served for fourteen years.

In addition, Ben's a writer and serves as a contributing editor to *Christianity Today* and *Leadership* and is author of *Waiting: Finding Hope When God Seems Silent* (InterVarsity).

Mastering a Role

To put it another way, unlike my early days in ministry, Paul Cedar doesn't need a haircut; Kent Hughes doesn't need a primer on good manners; Ben Patterson doesn't need a loan for new clothes. These men have not only mastered the basics, they are well on their way to mastering the pastoral role.

That's not something any of us will ever complete, of course. *Mastering* is an active participle, an ongoing process. We speak about great artists as "masters." But they frown when we do, because until their death, they are always frustrated that they've yet to master this technique or that.

Living the pastoral role is also an art, something that demands both intuition and practiced skill, and something that requires a lifetime to do well. We trust this book will help you in your life calling.

— *Mark Galli*
associate editor, LEADERSHIP Journal
Carol Stream, Illinois

PART ONE

The Dimensions of the Role

The pastorate is one of the few professions where the professional can aspire to be Renaissance person, someone who employs a number of skills and interests to serve God and neighbor.

— *Paul Cedar*

CHAPTER ONE

The Unique Role of the Pastor

After I'd pastored Lake Avenue Congregational Church for about a year, Peter Wagner said to me, "I think the two toughest jobs in the world are being President of the United States and pastor of Lake Avenue Congregational Church." I don't know that Lake Avenue was tougher than other pastorates, but I am convinced he was at least partially right. The pastorate is among the most difficult vocations today.

To begin with, pastors rarely see their work neatly and tidily wrapped up. Just before I entered seminary, a veteran Wesleyan

Methodist pastor took me by the arm and said, "There's one thing I enjoy in the ministry more than anything else."

He had a twinkle in his eye, so I knew he was setting me up. But I went for it: "What's that?"

"Saturday mornings. That's the morning I mow my lawn. It's the one thing I do every week where I can look back and see what I accomplished."

People are designed by God to receive satisfaction when they've accomplished a worthy task. Unfortunately, the pastorate is one of those vocations where the worthiest accomplishments — spiritual growth, for instance — are intangible. Bankers, carpenters, and printers get to see measurable, tangible results. But pastors often cannot. That can wear on them.

Add to that the constant daily pressures — sick to be visited, bulletins to be run, sermons to be written, hurt feelings to be soothed, church conflicts to be negotiated, budgets to be met, a community to be reached — and you've got a formula for rapid burnout.

It's not unusual for pastors to succumb in this environment. Some look to sexual gratification to give comfort; others simply give up and quit; others still just slowly wear themselves out. I know one minister, a man with a tremendous pastor's heart, whose ministry had a national reputation, who left the pastorate nearly a broken man. By God's grace he has experienced considerable psychological and spiritual healing and has bounced back. But he remains a living reminder of the difficulty of being a pastor.

This reality of the pastoral life can be dealt with in a variety of ways. Certainly a deep prayer life goes a long way toward maintaining vibrancy and health. Yet I've also found that reminding myself of the unique aspects of pastoral ministry renews me in my calling.

In my ministry, I've pastored Methodist, Evangelical Free, congregational, and Presbyterian churches, in both the Midwest and the West Coast. I've worked in small congregations and large, and now I'm president of a denomination. As I've worked in a variety of settings, I've noticed certain common denominators of pastoral life that demonstrate the uniqueness of the pastoral calling.

A Renaissance Calling

In an age in which specialists abound, the pastorate requires a wide variety of skills. It's one of the few professions where the professional can aspire to be Renaissance person, someone who employs a number of skills and interests to serve God and neighbor.

Pastors of smaller churches know this reality all too well. But even when I headed a church with a staff of seventeen, I believed it essential to encourage us all to remain generalists. Certainly, each staff person had his or her specialty. But I wanted each staff person to employ and constantly improve a variety of skills to accomplish his or her work.

For example, the pastor of music must be much more than an excellent musician. He or she must be a planner, coordinating worship activities with the senior pastor; a recruiter, inviting people to join choirs and orchestras; a people manager, directing a large number of people with a variety of ages and gifts; a financial manager, overseeing a significant budget; a master of ceremonies, leading public worship and congregational singing on special occasions; a negotiator, resolving conflicts and disagreements between people; and a pastor, caring for the members of the various musical groups of the church.

Now that's a Renaissance person! And other staff positions are no different.

Entrance into People's Private Lives

Few professionals in our society have an open invitation to their clients' personal lives. Nor do many have the opportunity to be with people during critical life passages: birth, illness, marriage, death.

But the minister does.

This is so characteristic of our vocation that we call ourselves *pastors*. Most of us see ourselves as shepherds who personally watch over our people, know them individually, and share in their private lives. That's a unique privilege we should never abandon.

Recently I visited a layman who is a national leader in his

denomination. Over the years, he has been deeply involved in his local church as well as his denomination. He is a churchman in the best sense of the term.

With tears in his eyes, he told me how badly neglected he was feeling. He recently had undergone surgery, and the pastor did not make a hospital visit nor telephone nor even write a personal note.

The man was crushed: "I feel as though I don't have a pastor. He is too busy with administration and preaching to care about people. I'm not the only one — many members of the congregation also are hurting because of the lack of pastoral care."

I understand the pastor's temptation to give himself fully to administration and preaching. Sometimes it feels like there's just too much to do. But we give up an essential ministry when we give up pastoral care. Pastoral care is not only one of the greatest needs of our fast-growing, impersonal society, it is also a unique privilege of the pastor.

Public Proclamation to Those We Love

Naturally, one of the distinctive callings of the pastor is public proclamation. Other professionals speak publicly on issues concerning people's lives, yet the pastor's proclamation is unique. Not only do we speak about eternal matters, but we speak to people we love. We don't preach to an audience nor to constituents but to brothers and sisters in the family of Christ. Each Sunday morning preachers look out on people they know and love.

When we forget that, our preaching becomes strained and impersonal. We're more likely to fill our sermons with "shoulds" and "oughts." We may start seeing the congregation as "them." That attitude can quickly turn ministry into a dreary business of correcting wayward sinners.

We rarely choose this preaching style intentionally. Instead, it sneaks up on us, especially when we're under pressure or when we overemphasize one aspect of preaching.

A couple of years ago, I received a letter from a couple in our congregation who begged me to start "loving them" from the pulpit rather than "scolding them." I'd been preaching a series of messages on the minor prophets; my messages were likewise prophetic, although appropriate for the congregation. But somehow, in spite of my sincerity and fine exegesis, my preaching had become unbalanced — at least in their eyes.

I was reminded that even prophetic preaching should be communicated with love and grace, not only in my words but in my attitude and spirit.

Proclaiming the Word, then, is a special form of communication that only pastors enjoy. Besides giving people the words of eternal life, we give care from the pulpit — public personal care.

Spiritual Counseling

The longer I'm in the ministry, the more firmly I believe in *pastoral* counseling. I was not always so enthusiastic about it, however.

When I was in seminary, in the middle 1960s, psychology was just finding its way into seminary curriculum. As we studied this specialty, many of us students, without realizing it, developed inferiority complexes about counseling. Studying psychological literature inclined us to think that only those specially trained in psychology could provide first-rate, professional counseling.

Along the way in ministry, however, I realized that psychological counseling, as important as it is, could never replace pastoral counseling. Pastors can introduce a distinctive feature into counseling: a spiritual perspective.

Naturally, any Christian psychologist can do the same. But people who come to a pastor for counseling are more likely seeking spiritual as well as psychological guidance. If they were most concerned about psychological dynamics, they would probably go elsewhere. But when they want to understand the spiritual root of their psychological troubles, they often come to a pastor.

While helping couples resolve problems like communication and finances, I've often found their deepest problem is spiritual. Without a fundamental change of attitude, all my tips for them getting along better will amount to nothing.

For example, one couple came to me for crisis counseling late one New Year's afternoon. I listened to their mutual accusations, and I was astounded when the wife began her complaints with their wedding day some twenty years before.

It became evident that the root problem was not her husband's faults or her domineering and caustic manner. Both of them needed the same thing — to follow Jesus as Lord, to allow the Holy Spirit to pour love and patience into them. Over a period of weeks, I saw both finally repent and begin building their marriage on Jesus Christ.

At other times, what troubled people need more than anything is forgiveness — a spiritual "commodity." They may need to learn communication skills and understand their past. But they also may need to be freed from resentment, or they may need to experience God's forgiveness themselves. In the counseling setting, the pastor is in a singular position to speak of God's forgiveness and to help people turn to Christ to help them forgive others.

I will never forget a young wife and mother who came to visit me several years ago. Her face was literally twisted in agony; she was carrying a burden that was destroying her. She shared with me something that she had never shared with anyone else:

While she was a teenager, she had become pregnant and had had an illegal abortion. Her parents had not known, nor had her friends, her husband, nor three children. She felt, though, she simply could not carry the burden any longer.

I had the privilege and delight of helping her ask God to forgive her. She was completely set free that morning by a loving and forgiving God. She left my study rejoicing and radiant. Never again did she have to look back at the burden of that sin.

So pastoral counseling has remained an important part of my ministry. In the larger church, I was limited as to how much counseling I could undertake. Nonetheless, even in a large church like Lake Avenue I made it a practice to see anyone who wanted to see me, although people might have to wait a few weeks for an appointment. I didn't want to give up this unique pastoral opportunity to help people integrate the spiritual and psychological.

Vision Casting

There are not many professionals who have the privilege of setting and maintaining vision for their organizations. The pastor is one of them.

Vision casting is not simply icing on the pastoral cake. The church's vitality depends on it. Lloyd Ogilvie at Hollywood Presbyterian Church used to talk about how some churches get in the habit of "clipping coupons on the past," recalling endlessly the glory days of a church. That can undermine the ministry of the church and be corrected only when the pastor makes use of this particular privilege.

In one church I served, the congregation paid a great price for looking back. The previous pastor had not cast vision for the future, so by the time I arrived, we were several years late in beginning a new building program. In the meantime, as our community exploded in population, our little sanctuary stood at capacity. We failed to incorporate a large number of new people during that window of opportunity.

Vision casting is also vital to the financial health of a congregation. When a church is facing a financial challenge or crisis, the pastor is often the only one who can give leadership to the congregation by communicating effectively the church's mission and the need for sacrifice. The pastor is the one who can keep the focus on ministry, as opposed to just raising funds.

I know of one congregation that was having trouble building a new sanctuary and sustaining their annual budget. Some trustees thought they should simply cut the budget. But the pastor convinced them they could raise the money if they communicated their situation honestly and candidly to the congregation.

So they did just that. In fact, the pastor became specific, tying the financial need to the mission of the church: "If we don't receive more, we'll have to cut back on one of the ministries of the church. In fact, we'll have to lay off one of the pastoral staff." When people saw the personal dimension of the problem and the ministry that would suffer, they perked up. They had a congregational meeting soon after that and in one night raised over half of the money they needed. A clear vision made a difference.

Laying before the church our mission is not only our privilege as pastors but an effective use of our pastoral position.

A Sacramental Presence

I don't understand it fully, and it doesn't always accord neatly with my Protestant theology, but it's a reality I've experienced repeatedly in ministry: Pastors have a sacramental presence in certain situations. I've seen it happen at weddings, funerals, the commissioning of missionaries, and the ordination of ministers. I've experienced it especially during dedications, baptisms, and Communion.

Whether one calls them *ordinances* or *sacraments* or *rites* doesn't matter. During such events, time touches eternity; the human and the sacred interact in a unique way. Although I fully affirm the priesthood of all believers, these are special moments in a pastor's ministry when he or she acts like a priest for the people. Some people seem to need another to represent God in such settings, and so the minister becomes an instrument, a vehicle to communicate God's presence and blessing at such times.

I find this is also true during people's crises. We can send deacons and deaconesses by the dozens to the hospital to visit, for instance, but the pastor has a unique relationship to a parishioner facing an operation. Whether it's good theology or not, people sense that a pastor represents God in a way other people do not.

For example, several years ago I visited parents whose son had just been killed in a motorcycle accident. I cried out to God, "Lord, what do I say? What do I do? How do I respond? If you're not possessing me, if you're not ministering through me, whatever I do is going to be inadequate. So guide me."

In such situations, I've sometimes said many words and sometimes few. But even more important than my words has been my pastoral presence. It's not that Paul Cedar was there; it's that a minister of the gospel was there. And it's not because I've gone as a religious professional but simply as a person publicly identified with God that people have been helped.

It's incredible, really, that God uses pastors in such ways.

But it's an unequaled reality of ministry.

Bird's Eye View of God's Grace

Finally, pastors, because of their particular role of overseeing the church, have the privilege of seeing God work time and again in the lives of people. Because we're involved in so many people's lives, we get to see not only their struggles but also the resulting victories and spiritual growth. It's not unlike a parent's perspective, seeing what God does in the lives of your children.

Not long ago, a young man met with me to discuss a new direction he and his family were exploring. As we talked, I was reminded where this man was spiritually a few years earlier, and again I was astounded at God's goodness.

He grew up attending church. His father died when he was a boy, and his mother, a godly woman, raised him alone. During the late 1960s, this young man rebelled against his mother and became a hippie, eventually living with a number of different girlfriends over the years.

The last girlfriend he lived with became pregnant. She was a woman he deeply loved, but still he was angry. He asked her to arrange an abortion. But then they both began to wonder if they wanted that.

As he thought about it, God began to work in his life. One Sunday he showed up at the church I was serving, and during the service God prompted him to redirect his life.

Shortly thereafter, he proposed to his girlfriend and married her, and they both started attending church. Eventually they both committed their lives to Christ and joined the church. After their daughter was born, I performed the dedication.

Four years later, I noticed this little girl during our church Christmas program, standing up front singing. I couldn't keep the tears back as I realized she was here only through God's gracious intervention.

Every Christian gets to enjoy watching God work in people. But in a pastor's life, that experience is multiplied by tens and twenties. It's just another example of the unique privileges we have in ministry.

Our vocation is our calling to serve Christ; our occupations are the jobs we do to earn our way in the world. While it is our calling to press our occupations into the service of our vocation, it is idolatrous to equate the two.

— Ben Patterson

CHAPTER TWO
A Call or Career?

I was kneeling on the steps of the chancel with several hands laid on my shoulder. The occasion was my ordination into the ministry, and the pastor was praying a seemingly interminable prayer for God's blessing and power to be upon me. My legs had started to cramp. Sweat was soaking through my black robe, a garment whose origins were in Northern Europe and whose wearer was in Southern California on a balmy May evening. And my knees felt as though they were piercing the scarlet carpet.

Does he think I need more prayer than usual? I thought. Then, as if in answer to my question, he prayed, "Lord, as Ben feels the weight of these hands upon his shoulders, may he feel the weight of what he has been called to do."

Amen.

"But may he feel also the strength of your everlasting arms bearing him up."

Amen and amen!

That is what ministry has been like ever since: an impossible, unbearable job accompanied by an improbable, inexplicable strength.

The apostle Paul took inventory of his vocation and asked, "Who is equal to such a task?" My version of that question comes several times a year as I step into the pulpit: *Patterson, I wonder, just what do you think you are doing here? Who are you, of all people, to tell several hundred people what God thinks?*

The question has struck me on other occasions, too. One Sunday a man from my checkered past came to see if the preacher was indeed the same Ben Patterson he had known years earlier. I'm sure he wondered what I was doing leading a service of worship. Seeing him and remembering my past, I wondered myself.

Countless hours I have sat with people crushed by life's weight. I have tried to convey something of the mercy and hope of Jesus. Verily, *Patterson, just what do you think you are doing here?*

I would have no right, no reason, no hope in ministry were it not for one thing: Almighty God, in his inscrutable wisdom, called me to it. That is all. He has willed it, not I.

Sovereignly, the Spirit blows where he wants, and he has blown me into the ordained ministry. Like the new birth, I was born into this thing not by the will of a man or an institution, but by the will of my Father in heaven.

Hearing a Call Is No Career Move

I often have puzzled over this thing we designate a "call." What is it? How does it come? How do you know when it does?

Much I do not understand, but there is one thing I am solidly convinced of: a call is not a career. The pivotal distinction between the two may be the most important thing we ever understand about the call of God, especially in these times.

The words themselves immediately suggest one difference. Our English word *career* comes from the French *carriere*, meaning "a road," or "a highway." The image suggests a course one sets out on, road map in hand, goal in sight, stops marked along the way for food, lodging, and fuel.

Looking back, we can speak of one's career as the road one took in life. But more often we speak of it as we look forward, as the path one chooses and plans to travel professionally, an itinerary charted and scheduled. The destination is primary. The roads are well-marked. The rest is up to the traveler.

A call, on the other hand, has no maps, no itinerary to follow, no destination to envision. Rather, a call depends upon hearing a Voice. The organ of faith is the ear, not the eye. First and last, it is something one listens for. Everything depends upon the relationship of the listener to One who calls.

Careers lend themselves to formula and blueprints, a call only to a relationship. A career can be pursued with a certain amount of personal detachment, a call never.

When Moses heard God call him to free the slaves in Egypt, he first responded as though he were presented with a career decision. Was he qualified? Did he have the proper experience and unique skills required by such an undertaking? He talked to God as though he were in a job interview: Who am I to do such a thing? What if the people don't follow? And doesn't God know that I am a poor public speaker?

All of this was irrelevant to God. All that mattered was that Moses believe God could be trusted when he said, "I will be with you."

In short, all that mattered was the call, and that Moses bind himself to the one who issued the call. There were no road maps, only the Voice.

Discerning the Right Voice

How do we know we are hearing God's voice and not merely the voice of our own aspirations, desires that themselves contain godly ambition and selfishness comingled? How do we sort God's voice out of the clamor of so many messages?

In *Wishful Thinking*, Frederick Buechner writes, "There are all different kinds of voices calling to you, all different kinds of work. And the problem is finding out which is the voice of God, rather than of society, say, or the super-ego or self-interest. By and large a good rule for finding out is this: The kind of work God usually calls you to is the kind of work, (a) that you need most to do, and (b) that the world most needs to have done. If you really get a kick out of your work, you've presumably met requirement (a), but if your work is writing TV deodorant commercials, the chances are you've missed requirement (b). On the other hand, if your work is being a doctor in a leper colony, you have probably met requirement (b), but if most of the time you're bored and depressed by it, the chances are you've not only bypassed (a) but probably aren't helping your patients much either. Neither the hair shirt nor the soft berth will do."

I like the way Buechner concludes: "The place God calls you to is the place where your deep gladness and the world's deep hunger meet."

Without both, you fail. I see too many people in church, in virtually every church I've been in, doing things that "ought to be done." But they don't like it, and it's just wearing them down, and there's a joylessness about the whole thing.

It's a failure to do something that "needs to be done" but to do it without joy; there's no gladness about the whole thing. Gladness isn't necessarily emotional bubbles as much as it is significance, meaning, purpose, seeing it as worthwhile. You can suffer and sacrifice and still be glad about it.

I think it's just as wrong to do something that needs doing and hate it as it is to just do something that you like but that doesn't really need to be done.

So my working theology of a call includes this sense of

gladness, trying to find the common ground between my deep gladness and the needs I see around me.

A Call Is Something You Listen For

The essential nature of the call is illustrated in a folk tale about a father and a son. They were traveling together to a distant city. There were no maps. The journey was to be long and rough, fraught with dangers. The roads were unmarked and mostly nonexistent. Only the wisdom and experience of the father would get him and his son to their destination.

Along the way, the boy grew curious. He wanted to know what was on the other side of the forest, beyond that distant ridge? Could he run over and look? His father said yes.

"But Father, how will I know whether I have wandered too far from you? What will keep me from getting lost?"

"Every few minutes," the father said, "I will call your name and wait for you to answer. Listen for my voice, my son. When you can no longer hear me, you will know that you have gone too far."

Ministry is not an occupation but a vocation. It primarily demands not professional credentials but the ability to hear and heed the call of God. And that simply requires that we stay quiet enough and close enough to hear his voice and be held firm in our impossible task by his everlasting arms.

The Place of Professional Realities

Only with this understanding of the call in mind do I consider the "career" elements of ministry. For only when I clearly see my work as a call can I handle these other matters faithfully.

For instance, there are the educational and denominational requirements that precede ordination. Hebrew, Greek, preaching proficiency, all the tests and ordination exams — they each become major rights of passage. In my denomination, tremendous value is placed on education and advanced degrees. (In fact, I've noticed as I've gotten older, I'm automatically called "Dr. Patterson" and, after I turned 40, much of my mail has been addressed to this same said person, even though I don't have a doctorate — and I don't have any nor plans to get one.)

The point is that the call doesn't take place in a vacuum. There are churches and individuals and requirements that God uses to prepare us for ministry. They must be attended to with a seriousness that befits one who is called.

Now that I'm ordained, other professional elements enter the picture. For example, I'm presently head of a pastoral staff. So I have to enter the fray of personnel issues, performance evaluations, salary levels, and housing allowances. These issues don't go away just because they are not central to the call. Again, for those called to ministry, these issues must be attended to responsibly.

In fact, I think of professional requirements and duties as household chores. Taking out the trash is not the most important part of family life, but things get messy if it's not done. If I take out the trash and do the dishes, they won't make home life great. But if I don't do them, the house starts to stink.

In a similar vein, J. I. Packer likens the theologian to a water treatment plant, which eliminates sewage from water. The plant doesn't necessarily make water taste good, but it keeps things from getting too bad.

In ministry, things like education and salaries and study leave can never guarantee a fruitful ministry. But if pastors don't take care of these chores, things start to stink. The best thing that education and professional standards can do is prevent disaster.

These things aren't unspiritual, but they're not the essence of the call. They are simply some of the unavoidable things pastors do because of the call.

The Peril of a Professional

Still, for all that, the far more common danger among pastors is to let such matters dominate their ministry, to think of ministry primarily as a career.

If we view our calling as a career, however, we reduce the servant of Christ to a vapid creature called "the professional." Well dressed and well spoken, armed with degrees, leadership savvy, management manuals, and marketing studies — all to be used for the good of the Kingdom, of course — we intend to make a mark on the world, gain a little respect for the profession, and shed forever the pastor's Rodney Dangerfield image.

Sensible and realistic, professionals expect the church to treat them like professionals and negotiate salary and benefits to match.

It is terrifying to realize that professional clergy can apply the skills and sophistication of their trade to build large, exciting, growing churches, and to do it all without believing anything.

"God deliver us from the professionalizers," says Minneapolis pastor John Piper. Echoing St. Paul, he asks, "Hasn't God made pastors the last in all the world? We are fools for Christ's sake; professionals are wise. We are weak; professionals are held in honor. . . . Professionalism has nothing to do with the essence and heart of the Christian ministry. . . . For there is no professional childlikeness, no professional tenderheartedness, no professional panting after God. . . . How do you carry a cross professionally? . . . What is professional faith?"

[margin note: ✳ cf 1 Cor 1:26-28]

Worst of all, careerism drives a wedge between the God who calls and the person who answers. It leads us to believe that our performance is more important than our person, that how we do in the ecclesiastical marketplace (and it is a marketplace) is more important than how we stand before God.

Careerism would give us confidence in ourselves where we ought to tremble and cry out for mercy. There is no place in the professional syllabus for a Paul who came to Corinth in weakness and foolishness, or for a Jeremiah who ate the Word of God only to get a terrible case of indigestion, or for a Jesus who ended his public life on a cross.

[margin note: 1 Cor 2:1-5]

The Untamed Call

Inherent in God's call is something fierce and unmanageable. He summons, but he will not be summoned. He does the calling; we do the answering.

"You did not choose me; I chose you," Jesus told his disciples. There is always a sense of compulsion, at times even a sense of violence, about God's call.

Struck blind on the road to Damascus, Paul said later, "Woe is me if I preach not the gospel."

Jeremiah complained that God had seduced him into his vocation, and wouldn't let him out, no matter how much it hurt: "If I say, 'I will not mention him or speak anymore in his name,' his word is in my heart like a fire, a fire shut up in my bones. I am weary of holding it in; indeed, I cannot."

Spurgeon saw the divine constraint as such a sure sign of a call that he advised young men considering the ministry *not* to do it if, in any way, they could see themselves doing something else.

At times we try to tame the call by equating a staff position in a church or religious organization with the call itself. But the call always transcends the things we may be forced to do to earn money, even if those things are done in the church. The same distinction we urge our people to note applies to us: our vocation in Christ is one thing, our occupations quite another.

Our vocation is our calling to serve Christ; our occupations are the jobs we do to earn our way in the world. While it is our calling to press our occupations into the service of our vocation, it is idolatrous to equate the two. Happy is the man or woman whose vocation and occupations come close. But it is no disaster if they do not.

If tomorrow I am fired from my job as pastor of New Providence Presbyterian Church and am forced to find employment in the Sunoco station down the street, my vocation would remain intact. I still would be called to preach. Nothing would have changed my call substantially, just the situation in which I obey it. As Ralph Turnbull points out, I may preach as the paid pastor of a church, but I am not being paid to preach. I am given an allowance so that I can be more free to preach.

At times we try to tame the call by "clericalizing" it. Seminary education does not qualify a person for the ordained ministry, nor does additional psychological testing and field experience. Naturally, these may be valuable and even necessary for the ministry, but none of them alone or in combination is sufficient.

No office or position can be equated with the call. No credential, degree, or test should be confused with it. No professional jargon or psychobabble can tame it. No training or experience or ecclesiastical success can replace it.

Patterson, just what do you think you're doing? My answer: Trying to follow the Voice.

Only the call suffices. Everything else is footnote and commentary.

The young minister and the seasoned pastor are, in some ways, worlds apart in their view of the church and practice of ministry — and that's okay.

— Kent Hughes

CHAPTER THREE

Seasons Change, and So Do Pastors

O ur youth pastor, Dennis, came to me recently. "I want to rappel off the church," he said, "off the fourth story!" It was to be a scene for a youth video he was making, he explained.

I could have easily said no. First, it was dangerous. (I like to give my staff room to fail, but this gave a whole new meaning to the idea.) Furthermore, people could criticize me for allowing such crazy activities. But he's a creative guy. He relates well to the kids, and this was a culturally hot item. In addition, he was young and could do it.

"Just check with the custodian," I said, "to make sure the rope won't come loose and the building won't be damaged."

So he did it. With a Santa Claus hat on his head, he backed off the roof of our four-story building and rappelled to the ground. The video was outrageous, and the kids loved it.

Rappelling off buildings, however, would not exactly impress the main people I minister to. That's how it should be. The young minister and the seasoned pastor are, in some ways, worlds apart in their view of the church and practice of ministry — and that's okay. Each faces unique frustrations and temptations, and each has unique opportunities to minister effectively to God's people.

I see my ministry as falling into two basic stages: early ministry, where I did youth work and then planted a church, and ministry now as head of staff. Here, then, are some insights I've gleaned about the hazards and opportunities of each stage of pastoral life.

Frustrations in Phases

Although my ministry has been fulfilling at each stage, I also see that each period also brings with it unique frustrations that, in the end, we simply have to learn to live with.

Lack of respect. When I was a youth pastor, I longed for congregational respect. I used to say I was more zoo keeper than pastor: as long as none of the animals got out of their cages, everybody was happy. That didn't do much for my self-esteem, and I felt alienated, like I was off in a corner with no significant role in the church.

That, in turn, nurtured a sort of reverse elitism: *The future of the church lies with the youth,* I'd think. *This is where it's happening. Everybody else is out of it!* That attitude, of course, didn't do much to get me the respect I longed for.

In fact, one advantage of early ministry aggravated the issue of respect. As a young pastor I enjoyed being close to people. I had considerable one-to-one contact, especially with youth and youth sponsors. But sometimes that very closeness diminished my profile as a pastor. When I became only "Hey you!" to people, they didn't perceive me as one having authoritative answers.

And it wasn't only the elders that didn't respect me. Often it was the kids I spent the most time with. At one youth gathering, I found myself under playful attack. "Hey! Let's try to drown the youth pastor!" was their gleeful battle cry. I spent much of the afternoon happily wrestling with some of my guys in the pool.

A few days later, though, I tried to speak with one of the boys I'd been wrestling with. He had been misbehaving in the youth group, and I had to confront him about it. But he wouldn't listen to me.

"I don't think you're so good," he said disrespectfully. "You're not a good husband to your wife or a good father to your kids. So get off my case!" I believe he spoke to me that way because I had become a little too familiar with him.

Another signal of lack of respect was the relatively meager administrative support I received. During my early years, I either had no secretary or one who merely worked part time, and I had to rely on old office equipment (or no equipment at all). That hampered my ability to administrate my work efficiently, and it raised my frustration level considerably some days.

The advantage of being a "junior pastor," of course, is that the buck doesn't stop at your desk. If the deacons became testy about a rappelling stunt or whatever, I just ducked. The criticism would fly by and land on my boss's desk. But during my early years of ministry, that plus didn't mitigate my frustration.

#2 *Administrative hassles.* Now that I'm further down the timeline, I have a vast arsenal of administrative tools at my disposal, but I also find the pace of change is frustratingly slow.

My youth group responded well and rapidly to change. They didn't ask all the what-if questions: "What if this happens? What if that doesn't work? What if we run out of money?" They were ready to get involved and take risks.

If I challenged them with, "All the heathen are lost," they would consider the matter seriously, saying, "Then I should change my life. I should join Operation Mobilization."

When presented with a challenge to change, the people I work with now are more likely to say, "But we've never done it that way before" or "How much did you say that was going to cost?"

Motivating an established church with an elaborate structure and a long, rich history can be like turning the Queen Mary around. You can turn a speedboat around on a dime. But it takes seven miles at sea to get an ocean liner headed in the opposite direction. And the older we become, the more likely we are to pastor ships instead of speedboats.

The time and energy that administration extracts from me also tends to separate me from my people. My maturity and leadership now give me the opportunity to make a large difference in many people's lives, but only if I'm willing to stay at the helm of the ship. Frankly, I'd like to be on the deck more often, chatting with the crew.

The Varied Pacing of Ministry

How we pace our ministries also changes over the years.

A holy impatience. When we're young, it's easier to be direct. We see clearly the problems of the church, and we have few qualms about telling people what ought to be done. We think, *This is right, and I know it's right. It's biblical, and this church needs it. So I'm not going to let anyone stand in my way.* So we barge through the front doors, trying to make change happen immediately.

Yes, sometimes we're brash and less than diplomatic. But it's that youthful impatience — especially if it's directed by biblical goals — that can often win the day.

In 1970 I became convinced that the *one great thing* our youth needed was involvement in missions. At that time short-term summer missions was not a common opportunity, especially for high schoolers. So I wrote missionaries and mission boards on every continent and compiled "103 Opportunities" that I grandly and with much fanfare presented to my kids.

The result? Fifty-five of them spent the summer of 1970 doing missionary work, and they were spread over five continents. It was a spiritual springtime for the church, although not the *one great answer* I had envisioned!

Younger ministers can get away with that type of holy drive, partly because congregations expect that from us when we're young. But as we mature in ministry, other character traits must emerge.

#2 *A godly patience.* The more at home I've become in the ministry, the more I use the back door. Instead of barging through the front door, guns blazing, I slip in quietly, unnoticed. I'll take someone out to lunch, listen respectfully, and in the process introduce my ideas in a noncombative mode, allowing others time for thought.

I'm also more comfortable with the fact that my plans won't get accepted immediately. Getting College Church into a major building program without sinking the church has been a huge exercise in patience. I didn't just stand up one day and announce that we needed to build a $6.5 million structure. I had to lay the groundwork for years.

It began, in fact, when the congregation held a meeting to discuss air conditioning. Many people were saying, "Why should we install air conditioning? It's unbearable only ten Sundays out of the year. We'll still come to church." I had to remind them that a restaurant operating that way would go out of business.

In time I got them to see that we were trying to reach others besides the already committed. Patience paid off. We got the air conditioning, and now, years later, we're building new facilities.

I may have to settle for accomplishing only a small part of the plan at the beginning of a new venture. But if it moves the church in the right direction, in a year or two the whole program can be in place.

Temptations in Time

In each stage of ministry, my spiritual life has been tested differently.

#1 *Vulnerability to flattery.* I didn't get to preach much as a youth pastor. But if someone came up after my sermon and said, "That was great! Do you know what we need around here? We need to hear more of you," I tended to believe them.

Yeah, you're right, I'd think. *That is exactly what this church needs:*

more of me. When young, we're more vulnerable to such flattery.

Now I know the difference between compliments and flattery. If a long-time member tells me, "Pastor, that was a good sermon Sunday," that's one thing. But it's another when someone who's been attending but three weeks says, "Boy! That was the best sermon I have ever heard!" Then my red flag goes up. It could be that they've never heard good preaching, but more likely they are flattering me to get my attention.

I've learned, then, to be cautious over the years. Experience has shown me the truth of what Solomon says — to be wary of flatterers.

Vulnerability to security. As one gets on in ministry, I've witnessed an increasing temptation to play it safe, to become vulnerable to the need for security, to see risk as a young man's game. The more one achieves professionally, the more one has to lose and the greater the instinct to play it safe. That's why some pastors are tempted to pad their boards with supportive "yes people" and hire staff who don't threaten them.

I have consciously fought this instinct by surrounding myself with superior people, many with abilities exceeding mine. I invite them to push and ask hard questions. I allow them to spread their wings, to try new programs and fresh ideas. And when they fly, I fly — and flying is risky business!

Pastoral Care in Two Dimensions

The essence of ministry — pastoral interaction with people — also changes with the years. The same ministry gets done, but in two different ways.

Pastoral contact. As a youth pastor, my phone rang constantly. I was available all the time. When I became the pastor of a small church, I involved myself in everything: Sunday school, the youth program, evangelism. Since I worked closely with everyone, they all knew me. We built the new church building together; we cleaned toilets together. People had no compunctions about calling me at any time.

Because of that close contact with people, I could invest myself into individual lives with great energy and good results.

In my early pastorate, I coached a soccer team, "The Awesome Aztecs," and some of my players came from Jewish, Mormon, and Hindu homes. We had a great time together all season. To thank me for my efforts, the team along with their parents came to church one Sunday, and they all sat on the front row.

Pastoral oversight. When I came to College Church, I suddenly had ten times more people to pastor, but I received only a third of the phone calls. The older minister usually has more responsibility, so people say, "Well, we shouldn't call pastor at home. We should wait till tomorrow morning." And sometimes they simply don't trouble me with their problems. It's sad, but some people no longer consider me approachable.

Then again, even when people do ask for pastoral attention, my varied responsibilities force me to weigh my response. A woman recently asked me, "My husband and I are having trouble. Would you counsel us regularly?"

"I can counsel you a couple of times, but then I will have to refer you," I explained. "And if you need some financial assistance, we can help with the first five or six sessions."

I know that if I take even two or three people on for regular counseling, it will demand my full attention. I still counsel people, but not as much as I used to.

I simply no longer have the luxury of being involved with as many people. If I were to do so, I wouldn't administrate well; I wouldn't adequately prepare sermons. As an older pastor with more responsibility, I have to work through other people.

The irony is that although I personally give less pastoral care, more people receive individual attention. I administrate staff people who visit hospitals, counsel, and make calls into homes. Our church also offers courses that train lay people to give pastoral care to one another.

So although I'm frustrated by administration, my frustration is tempered by the fact that I can oversee the pastoral care of hundreds of people.

Learning to Preach

One of the greatest challenges of ministry is to communicate the Good News to people. It's a complex task, and not every part of it can be perfected at once. In fact, we should not burden ourselves trying to do at 25 what others are doing at 55. I've noticed, in fact, that different stages of ministry lend themselves to mastering different parts of the preaching process.

#1   • *Learning to be relevant.* When I got out of seminary, I entered ministry armed with all kinds of theological words. I was self-consciously bookish.

But that didn't compute into the world of youth ministry. Kids may be the most challenging group to relate to. They're a demanding audience. They're not going to let you get away with being irrelevant. They want fast-paced, graphic, honest dialogue. You can get away with boring adults, but kids won't tolerate it.

I had to learn, then, to relate to kids on their level. My wife says my vocabulary went through a complete transformation in about a month. So I spent my early ministry years learning how to translate the gospel into contemporary terms.

In fact, I've come to believe that youth ministry is the best place to learn how to do that. If you can communicate with teenagers, you can communicate with anybody. As a youth pastor, I learned many speaking techniques that I still draw on today.

#2   • *Crafting and precision.* In recent years my homiletical style has evolved even further. With collegians I could sit on the floor and dialogue from notes written on the margins of my Bible. When I pastored a small church, I began to construct outlines with greater substance and structure. Now I write out a complete manuscript, even if I don't use it in the pulpit. My people understand more nuances of biblical truth, and I must be clear and precise about how I communicate.

So in this stage of ministry, I'm constantly learning how to craft my sermons. I'm much more fastidious about exegesis and even the use of language. This is not something I had time to do when I was younger. Even if I did have time, I'm not sure it would have been worth the effort. Now it is, not only because I've already learned to be relevant but because my people expect it.

The Changing Focus of Ministry.

How I give my energies to ministry has also changed over the years.

#1 *A singular passion.* When I first started out, I thought I could change the world with my youth program. During the 1960s we sat on the floor for Bible studies, strummed guitars, and sang Jesus songs. We thought that was the answer for the whole church. If people would just sit on the floor and sing Jesus songs, they'd became like the church God intended.

That single-issue focus stayed with me into my early years as a pastor. I'd say to myself, *If I can get Evangelism Explosion going, then the church will turn around.* I'd preach with confident zeal, imagining one great sermon alone would impact my people for life. As a young minister, I would often devote myself fully to one thing, hoping it would make a big difference.

Early in ministry, we have the luxury and opportunity to have a narrow focus. That focus allows us to give programs the detailed attention and energy they need — especially if they are being created *ex nihilo*. And although my grandiose hopes for each program may have been misplaced, they each in their own way made a difference.

For example, in my first pastorate, I instituted an intern program for those considering going into the ministry. This not only provided interested people with ministry opportunities, they also received a modest amount of instruction in practical theology, which I taught weekly. The program continued for over a decade after I moved on.

#2 *A concern for complexity.* As my responsibilities in ministry changed, I began to see another dimension: the church wasn't one thing but many, and it was the coordination of the many that would, over the long run, make for effective ministry. Even after great sermons, I found myself realizing, *That may have been one of the best sermons I've ever preached, but alone it won't make any major difference. I've got to keep paying attention also to the other parts of the church's life — pastoral care, administration, and teaching.*

To put it another way, I no longer can evaluate rappelling off the church only in terms of what it can do for the youth. I also must consider how it might impact the ladies' missionary guild or the church's insurance coverage.

Complexities can clutter the big picture and make ministry decisions much harder. Then again, learning to look beyond the single ministry focus has also lowered my fear of failure. I've discovered that just as one sermon will not change history, one mistake will not collapse the kingdom of God. One bad program will not sabotage the church or destroy my ministry.

Rewards at Every Stage

On my dresser, where I can see it every morning, sits a picture of five guys, with sunglasses and slicked-back hair, on a 1968 Colorado River trip. That picture reminds me of what happened the next day, when four of them prayed with me to receive Christ. And it didn't end there.

One of those guys, Rick Hicks, went on to direct Forest Home, a Christian conference center in Southern California, and he recently received a Ph.D. To know that something I did as a youth pastor had lasting impact, to know that more than twenty years later those guys are still committed, pursuing ministries themselves and changing lives for Christ — that is wonderful. Seasons may change, as do pastors, but the rewards are essentially the same.

The rewards, of course, continue to unfold. Recently, I received this note from a junior high girl:

Dear Pastor Hughes,

After listening to your sermon today, I recommitted myself to our Lord. I have recently discovered myself just "going through the motions." I have since done devotions and witnessing to people. Your sermon spoke to me. Normally, I must confess, I don't listen very well. Today I did and you had a lot to say. I'm sure you spoke to many nonbelievers in our congregation. I have decided, if possible, to become a member of College Church (although I am only 13 years old and the only one in my family to go to this church). If you would like to get in touch sometime, my number is. . . . Thanks for your time.

Your sister in Christ,

Elizabeth

As Ecclesiastes puts it, there is a time for every season under heaven. That's certainly been true of my ministry. Each season of ministry has its liabilities and opportunities, but in each season God has been faithful, and his work has moved forward.

PART TWO

The Pastor and the Congregation

Leadership means action, not reaction. Yet the action we take must be responsive to the needs around us and to the leading of the Holy Spirit within us.

— Paul Cedar

CHAPTER FOUR
Leading or Responding?

When the phone rang one Sunday afternoon a few years ago, I thought it would be the chairman of the church board, telling me if the congregation in which I had recently candidated had voted me in as their pastor. When I answered the phone, the man at the other end of the line identified himself and said, "Pastor Cedar, I'm chairman of the reorganization committee at the church, and I want to welcome you as our new pastor."

"Well, thank you," I said hesitantly. "But the truth is, I haven't accepted the call yet. I haven't even heard the results of the congregational vote."

"Of course, I know it isn't official yet," he continued, "but I just wanted to invite you to meet with our committee. As you know, presently some nine separate church boards and committees oversee the life of our church. Frankly, sometimes it's been a struggle to coordinate nine separate boards and committees. Well, when the previous pastor left, he asked the leadership of our church to make a gift to our new pastor — a reorganized church structure. Hence our committee."

A few days later, after I accepted the call to that church, I met with the committee and listened to their various suggestions. Before long, it became clear that the committee was deadlocked. All eyes were soon on me.

"What it comes down to, Pastor Cedar," said the committee chairman, "is that you're the guy who has to work with the new structure. If you'll just tell us what you want, I believe the rest of the committee will be unanimous in supporting that plan." All around the room voices murmured and heads nodded in agreement.

"Brothers," I said, "that's a very gracious offer. But let me make a counter offer. Let's not change things just yet. I'd like to test drive this nine-committee structure for a few months and see how she handles. That'll give me a chance to get acquainted with the congregation, the staff, and the leadership, as well as time to pray. By then, I should have a better sense of what would be best, not only for me but for this church."

I asked them not to disband the committee but just to take a recess. At the end of six months, I would ask them to reconvene.

I could have taken a strong, authoritarian leadership role at that point. Change was needed, but the church wasn't ready yet for radical restructuring. They first needed a "servant leader" who, under the leading of the Great Shepherd, would try to be sensitive to their needs.

After six months, I had a much better feel for the pulse of the church — what issues were important, where feelings ran high, who stood guard over which patches of turf. We did a study of the committees and discovered that over half of them had no real idea of their charter. Almost two-thirds of our committees had no idea to whom they were accountable. The only reason the whole structure worked was that it was peopled by godly men and women who did their best to carry on the ministry humbly, diligently, and without grasping for power or recognition.

So I asked a friend who was a leader in the church to head up a series of congregational forums to receive input into the restructuring process. At one of these forums, I stood before the people and said, "I've been with you for half a year, learning and listening and observing. Now, because God has called me to be in leadership among you, it's time to share with you my vision for the shaping of our church ministry.

"To be frank, I would find it impossible to sit on nine ruling boards in this church," I said. "However, I think I can live with three boards. So that's what I propose: first, a board of trustees; second, a board of nurture; and third, a board of mission, evangelism, and outreach."

At that point, someone stood up and asked, "Well, what if we have five boards?"

I think I surprised the questioner and the rest of the congregation with my reply: "I simply cannot give leadership to more than three church boards. I'm not trying to be difficult. I'm trying to be honest with you about my own gifts and limitations as a church leader."

At the conclusion of the process, which consisted of a number of public forums over many weeks, a unanimous vote of the congregation endorsed the three-board proposal. We restructured and moved on.

Throughout that process, I exercised different forms of leadership. Initially, I responded — listening and learning. Ultimately, I had to stake out a position in a forceful, dramatic way because the congregation needed to understand the seriousness of the situation and my feelings about it.

Through this and other experiences, I've learned (often the hard way) that there are times to lead and times to listen, times to implement my dreams and times to invite others to dream, times to initiate and times to wait for ideas to percolate up from the laity. The key, I believe, is to be sensitive to the leading of Christ, the head of the church.

The Challenge of the Culture

We live in a society that chafes under leadership. We are a nation of rugged individualists, fiercely independent. This independent spirit has also infected the church, making it difficult and often frustrating to be a church leader.

This nettlesome truth was brought home to me toward the end of my tenure at one church I served. I became convinced that our church should have a mission statement to set forth our purpose. I also felt that the basic component of the mission statement had to be the Great Commission.

But when I went to the appropriate committee with this proposal, I encountered a surprisingly strong wall of resistance. It wasn't that anyone was overtly hostile or abusive, but some people became emotional at the thought of an overarching focus for our ministry.

"The idea of a mission statement sounds so confining and restrictive," said one man. "You're being unreasonable, Paul," said another. "People will never accept that," said another still.

I tried to make the case that there was plenty of room for diversity and experimentation within the bounds of a basic mission statement. I also explained that such a statement would give our church a premise and focus for ministry. I argued that our people could function much more effectively within a framework. But with feelings running high over the issue, the dialogue quickly bogged down.

Some didn't want the Great Commission as the basis of the statement. Others wanted no statement at all. Still others proposed draft statements I felt were worse than no statement at all. After a few months, the process petered out, in large part because I was called to a new ministry.

The disagreement over this issue — an issue I championed out of deeply held convictions — was between sincere, well-intentioned Christians. But I felt that much of the resistance resulted from a cultural mindset that says, "I don't want anyone to tell me what to do. I don't want anyone or anything to limit my options."

Given this environment, which can be found anywhere in America, I've found it best to exercise what I call "responsive leadership."

Not long ago, a friend asked, "As a leader in the church, do you see yourself essentially as an initiator or a responder? How would you describe your leadership style?" After reflecting on some of the key leadership decisions of my career, I concluded that I'm both an initiator and a responder.

I see a biblical leader as a responsive leader but not a reactive leader. There's a big difference between the two. To be responsive means to be sensitive and attuned to people's concerns and, at the same time to be sensitive to the leading of the Holy Spirit. To be reactive means to be controlled and compelled by people and situations.

It's easy to fall into the trap of reacting — to pressures, to conflict, to crises and brush fires. When I have inadvertently done that, I felt less like a leader and more like a pinball. Leadership means action, not reaction, yet the action we take must be responsive to the needs around us and to the leading of the Holy Spirit within us.

Most of us function somewhere between the two extremes my friend suggested. And many have had a chance to take a personality inventory or a leadership test, giving us an awareness of where we lie on the assertiveness spectrum. But no matter what our natural tendencies, we recognize there are both times to lead and times to respond, and times to lead responsively.

When to Lead

Two circumstances in particular signal me to take charge, as W. C. Fields once said, to "take the bull by the tail and face the situation."

When I have a strong Bible-based and Spirit-led conviction about something. Naturally, not every issue about which I have strong opinions qualifies. But sometimes the Spirit creates a conviction within me, and I know it's time to lead.

During the return leg of a tour I led to Australia and New Zealand, I had just such an inspiration. I was walking alone on one of those pristine beaches of the South Pacific, not another soul in sight. As I walked and prayed, God, I believe, put an idea into my mind, complete in most of its details. I felt that the church I served should have a new ministry to baby boomers.

At the time, our church provided no worship tailored to the needs of this group, especially those who had become Christians during the Jesus movement of the 1960s and '70s. Some of these Christians truly wanted to be a part of our worship but balked at our formal hymns, organ music, and choir anthems.

So I took my new inspiration back to the States and, because of my deep conviction, gave strong leadership to the concept. Opposition arose from sincere traditionalists within the church who felt, for example, that the church's music had to be Bach played on organ. They felt there was no room in the church for any other kind of worship experience. I never doubted their motives, yet I patiently and persistently asserted my conviction that we had room in our Sunday evening schedule to create a new kind of worship.

We began by offering a mixture of hymns, worship songs, and contemporary music, performed with synthesizer, guitars, drums, and other instruments. Instead of the usual twenty-five-minute sermon, we had a teaching and exposition that went from forty to fifty minutes. We replaced the formal benediction with a time of open prayer, when people could pray alone or in groups, in the pews or kneeling at the altar. The response was tremendous — not only did bunches of baby boomers attend, but many experienced Christ for the first time.

Although at the beginning, I had to give leadership to this issue on faith, in the end events bore out my impression that the Spirit had given me this conviction, making me grateful I had asserted my leadership.

When there is sin, error, falsehood, malfeasance, or misbehavior in the church. There is a prophetic dynamic to the pastoral role, although like most pastors I'm often reluctant to take it up. We pastors rightly highlight grace, forgiveness, and love. But sometimes I must speak the truth in love.

I recently learned about an incident in which an associate pastor of a large church took a group of parishioners on a tour of mission projects in Europe and Africa, projects the congregation was supporting. These church members were to come back and report to the congregation.

Upon the group's return, the senior pastor was told that some members of the group, including the associate pastor, had imbibed alcoholic beverages on the trip, and several people had become intoxicated.

Not wanting to prejudge the people involved, the senior pastor went to his associate, described the report he had received, and asked if the report was true.

The associate became defensive. "Nobody in this church is required to swear an oath of temperance," he said. "I don't think one Christian should decide for other Christians whether they should drink. It's a matter of Christian freedom."

"If you or anyone else in this church wants to take a drink as an individual," replied the senior pastor, "that's between you and your own conscience. But on a tour representing this church and the body of Christ, you give up your individual freedom. If you are not willing to submit your freedom to the good of this church and the reputation of the church, then there will be no more tours in the future."

Somebody has to lead the local church. You can't always have unanimity. You can't always have harmony. Decisions have to be made, and sometimes those decisions are painful or unpopular. The best any pastor can do is to try to respond to the Spirit's leading, submit decisions to the light of Scripture, continue listening and learning, and amid all of these tensions, move on.

When to Respond

Just as some circumstances signal it's time to lead, certain circumstances signal me it's time to respond. Let me note two.

When entering a new situation.

During my first few weeks at one church, many people in the congregation took me to lunch or dinner to get acquainted. In one instance, I was at lunch with a man I'll call George. Just after we had been served our salads, he got down to business.

"I've a question to ask you," he said. "My wife and I began attending this church just two weeks before the previous pastor left. We were really disappointed when he announced his departure. But we waited out the year and a half interim because we wanted to find out what direction the new pastor would lead the church.

"So that's my question: What are your goals? What are your plans? Frankly, if we like your answers, we're going to stay. If not, we'll go someplace else, because we feel that would be better for both us and the church."

"I agree completely," I said, "and I appreciate your candor. Of course, I hope and pray you'll want to take part in the future of our church. But the fact is, I don't have any program goals or ministry plans for this church right now.

"Frankly, I'm not concerned about my plans for this church. My commitment is to seek the leadership of the Lord of the church and then to lead the congregation in following our Lord. In short, my major goal is to seek and do the will of God, personally and as a church family."

A new situation signals me it's time to respond rather than initiate. George respected that, and from that day forward, he was one of the closest, most supportive, most delightful members of our congregation.

When confronted with a secondary issue. Secondary issues are not unimportant, but they are issues that Scripture deals with only vaguely or not at all; they are not core doctrines of the faith or essential mission priorities. Ironically, it's these peripheral issues that can tear a church apart.

Issues such as abortion and nuclear arms are argued fervently, with believers on both sides pointing to biblical principles and

passages for support. Other such issues include, "Should we belong to the National Association of Evangelicals?" or "Should we
drop 'congregational' from the name of our church?" "Yet on these
and many other issues no simple thus-sayeth-the-Lord pronounce-
ment exists in Scripture.

Perhaps the thorniest, most divisive issue is a building program. The debates can range from "How do we raise three million
dollars for a new sanctuary?" to "What color should the roof shin-
gles be?" Tragically, people often stake out positions on such issues
as if they were defending the deity of Christ.

Whenever I get caught in a crossfire over secondary issues, I
try to listen and learn before leading. As I mentioned above, there
are times when the Spirit leads me to take a strong stand. But my
usual course, at least at the beginning of discussions on secondary
issues, is to listen.

Although there are times to firmly lead and other times to
simply respond, most of the time I find a combination the most
effective approach. I call it leading responsively, and it has at
least five dimensions: stepping into ministry gaps, keeping people
in mind, remaining cautious about using authority, maintaining
accountability, and pacing leadership under pressure.

I. Step into Ministry Gaps

One church I served believed strongly in missions — it had a
large mission budget. Yet, as I examined this budget item by item, I
discovered that less than $1,000 of this immense sum was spent on
missions within our own community. In terms of its missionary
outreach, the church was a lighthouse in the world but only a night-
light at home.

At first I wondered if this fact signaled resistance to local
ministry. But the more I talked to people, the more I found a
genuine eagerness to reach the needs in our own backyard. So I
gave leadership to building up our local missions effort. We
prayed, planned, set goals, and met our goals. Within a year, we
had a significant budget slated for community outreach. Mean-
while, scores of church members became involved in specific

ministries in our own community.

Throughout my time as pastor of that church, I never heard a single word of criticism of our community outreach — not one! In this case, the church was just waiting to be led. But first I had to listen and look to both the people and the Spirit. Only then did I perceive a gap in the church's ministry. In the end, I led strongly but only in response to what I had discovered.

In many instances, then, congregations want to be involved and committed. They want goals to shoot for. Christians are eager to be God's vehicle for ministry in the marketplace, the suburb, the ghetto, the barrio, and around the world. They just need someone to examine their ministry and point the way to new opportunities.

Lead with People in Mind

Naturally, pointing the way is a complex process. But I've found that by following four guidelines — each of which responds to fundamental needs and concerns of people — I have a much better chance of helping people move ahead:

1. *Set goals within a time frame of not more than one year*. I believe this is good advice in many spheres but especially the church. Most people simply cannot envision a five-year span but can readily digest planning for a year.

2. *Set measurable goals with visible, tangible results*. For example, one may want the singles' ministry to grow from fifty to seventy within nine months. That's a goal that can be easily measured. People are encouraged and motivated to greater effort when they see progress in meeting goals.

3. *Create an open process or forum, where the members can voice their feelings and ideas*. In order to be involved and motivated, people need to feel a sense of ownership and identification with the plans and goals. Moreover, members are a valuable source of creative ideas.

4. *Examine all the options*. I try to put everything on the table for discussion. For example, rather than assuming the church must begin a massive building program, it is wise to consider other possibilities —expansion of present facilities, church plant-

ing, satellite churches, among others.

I've found when leadership gets too far out in front, people seldom follow. But when people feel they are a part of the team, that they are taken seriously, then great things begin to happen. That's also part of responsive leadership.

Be Cautious About Using Pastoral Authority

One church I served has always been a praying church, with a strong emphasis on corporate prayer. During my tenure, we had quarterly all-church nights of prayer. I found that when we made the usual announcement of an upcoming night of prayer, we would get a turnout of around two to three hundred people. But when I forcefully asserted my pastoral leadership from the pulpit and promoted my vision for corporate prayer, hundreds of additional people turned out.

At first, I was ecstatic to see this great desire for prayer. And I would share my excitement with others at the prayer meetings, only to discover that many in the congregation were not nearly as excited. Then I realized that many people were coming for the wrong reason. They were following my leadership, coming to please me, but they weren't coming with hearts prepared to pray.

God opened my eyes at that point. I realized I might have actually encouraged our people to honor God with their lips while their hearts were far from him. Clearly, I needed to back off and figure out what my people understood about prayer before I led boldly in prayer again.

Part of responsive leadership, then, is to be cautious about using one's authority. In short, we need to invite people to follow us as we follow Christ.

Maintain Accountability

During my tenure at Lake Avenue Congregational Church, we built a building that to some people seemed too big. The price tag was enormous — in money, administrative hassles, and energy. But most of the church believed it was a case of evangelize or perish. So I led the church out of its comfort zone, and fortunately, we didn't fall into the Twilight Zone. By God's grace, we survived and grew.

Yet, we leaders may confuse our own agendas and ambitions with God's plan for the church. It's easy to fool ourselves into thinking we want God's glory when all the while we only glorify ourselves. I've seen many pastors stumble into that snare, bringing enormous pain upon themselves and their congregations. These are generally pastors who operate with a large degree of autonomy, having little or no accountability to a board of elders, to the congregation, or to anyone else.

Over the years, I became convinced that as I led, there had to be some mechanism to give me counsel. I found that my ideas for leading the church were nurtured and strengthened by the input of others in a group process. I didn't want to surround myself with a circle of "yes men" but with a few people of maturity, honesty, and boldness, willing not only to affirm me but to challenge me as well. While at Lake Avenue I met with a kitchen cabinet, a group of people who could perform this function for me. They helped me keep my leadership responsive.

Some of the most profound insights that affected my ministry have come from very simple, humble people in the church. It's often God's pattern to speak through those unexpected people of unfeigned faith.

For me, then, responsive leadership requires I be accountable to others, both formally and informally.

Paced Leadership Under Pressure

Perhaps the most difficult time to know when to lead and when to respond is during conflict. Emotions run high. Thinking and response time shrinks, and it becomes easier to make a poor decision.

I don't like conflict. I didn't deal with conflict to any great degree until I became an adult. So I entered the ministry with a sort of Camelot image of what the church should be and how Christians should act. Whenever I encounter angry, confrontational people in the church, it's always an uncomfortable experience. Even after years in ministry, I'm still on a learning curve.

During conflict, then, I tend to want to hurry up and find a solution. When I do that, though, I usually find myself enmeshed in even more conflict, now over what the solution should be. Instead, I've found that, at the outset, listening usually should take precedence over decisive action.

One of the most painful tests of my ability to lead during conflict came a number of years ago. The problem involved a fellow staff member whom I had come to love and respect deeply. He was a gifted individual, but the church ministry had evolved to a point where his gifts were no longer needed in the area where he was serving. The board and I, after months of agonizing, decided to ask him to move to another area of the church's ministry, for which he was well qualified. The move was not a demotion, nor was there any decrease in salary or benefits. In our minds, we had found the perfect solution. Unfortunately, he didn't see it that way.

Although I did not become aware of the problem for months, this associate began criticizing me behind my back, telling others that I had fired him, that I had malicious motives, and on and on. By the time I became aware of the stories, he had already aroused a large number of his own constituents in opposition to me. I was absolutely shocked. I thought he was happy in his new position. I never imagined such a thing could happen.

In this situation, I felt it best first to bring together everyone affected by the problem and get the issues aired out. So I encouraged the church board to call an open forum of the congregation, believing that the evening would surely conclude with forgiveness, reconciliation, and celebration.

During that meeting, however, several people stood up and made angry, ugly, irrational accusations against me and other leaders. These were people I had respected, loved, and considered friends. Yet I suddenly learned they had long been harboring grievances against me, based on unsubstantiated rumors and false impressions. Suddenly, I didn't know who in that room was my friend and who would be the next to rise up and accuse me.

One woman, whom I had always considered a supportive

friend, stood up, eyed me coldly, and said, "I think we're firing the wrong person here."

I was devastated, practically paralyzed. I didn't know how to lead, what to do, or what to say. Should I defend myself? Should I restore the staff member to his previous job?

He had assassinated me both in private and in public. I was angry and hurt. I felt betrayed by this man. Yet, paradoxically, I also wanted to reach out to him, to tell him that there was a terrible misunderstanding.

In the end, to keep from saying anything negative about him, I essentially said nothing at all. At the time, it seemed like the Christlike thing to do.

In retrospect, I should have become calmly assertive. Not that I should have vindicated myself, attacked the staff member, or mowed down my accusers. But I should have set the record straight, graciously, guilelessly, and candidly. I should have put the misconceptions and misinterpretations of these critics into a more realistic perspective.

More than any other time, then, conflict calls for responsive leadership. We must listen to hurts and grievances but then take control when a situation gets out of hand, especially when people succumb to gossip or assassinate character or call another's motives into question.

Our Pattern in Leadership

Some years ago, I had a discussion about leadership with another pastor, a gray-haired septuagenarian with fifty years of ministry under his belt and a dry sense of humor. "You know, Paul," he said, "I've never had a negative vote in a congregational meeting in all my years of ministry." I could tell by his wry grin and the twinkle in his eye that he was setting me up, but I had to ask anyway.

"How do you do it?" I said.

"Well, I moderate every meeting. And every time we have a vote on anything, I say, 'All in favor say, "Aye." ' And they say,

'Aye.' Then I say, 'Unanimously carried,' bang my gavel, and move on. It's foolproof."

I'm still not certain if he was serious. I'd prefer to think he was putting me on, because I'm convinced sometimes we need those nay votes.

Leadership means taking initiative. But leadership also means keeping our eyes and ears open to the Lord and his people, asking others to hold us accountable, continually testing our ideas in the crucible of debate and life experience, constantly observing and correcting, always eager to absorb new information and new ideas.

Most of all, leadership means being responsive to our ultimate leader, Jesus Christ. Jesus said he came not to do his own will, not to promote his own agenda, but to do the will of the Father. Christ is our pattern for responsive leadership.

Pastors must be pastors. But we must be people also.
— *Ben Patterson*

The Performance Factor

I felt a little ashamed of myself for doing it, but not enough to stop myself. It was my day off; my wife and I had taken our usual long walk, had breakfast together, and stopped in a clothing store to do a little shopping. When I saw two church members in the shop, I quickly ducked behind a mannequin, and when they weren't looking, I slipped out of the store. I was tired; it was my day off; I didn't feel like extending any greetings.

It wasn't pastoral of me, but it was honest. And it illustrates a struggle I face in the pastorate — trying to balance the tension between being the person I am and being that person called a "pastor."

Other professions live with the same tension, but they can handle it more efficiently. In *The Christian Century* magazine, columnist Martin Marty once wrote about the schizo-like attitude of flight attendants. On airplanes we find attendants gracious, sometimes to the point of gushiness. They look us in the eye, give us a big smile, and extend plenty of hospitality.

But when our flight lands and we spot these same attendants in the concourse or baggage claim area, they simply walk by, avert eye contact, and ignore us. Marty calls that "civil inattention." It's time for them to step out of the flight attendant role and be themselves.

Pastors must be pastors. But we must be people also. Although we can't divide our roles as cleanly as does a flight attendant, we still must figure out why and how to live with this tension. Here are some insights that have helped me.

There's More to Life Than Being Genuine

As a child of the 1960s, I wanted no part of the institutional baggage of the church. Even when I attended seminary, I intended to go into youth work. Ministry to me meant parachurch, non-ordained ministry. Like Father MacKenzie, one of "all the lonely people" in the Beatles' song "Eleanor Rigby," the pastors I knew seemed to be lonely, hollow men trapped in ecclesiastical roles, creatures weighted down with the expectations of their congregations' collective psyches. I believed that what they were forced to be kept them from what they ought to be — themselves, whatever that was.

I've gone through a few changes since then. I've learned that ministry is more than simply being myself, that in fact, ministry is often enhanced when I accept the pastoral role. In particular, there are five advantages of living in the pastoral role:

● *It checks individualism.* In an effort to be genuine, I sometimes think, *I'm going to say what I think and do what I want, regardless of people's expectations.* But sometimes people's expectations — for example, that pastors be good listeners or that pastors not selfishly pursue their own agendas — are exactly what a strong-headed person like me needs to adhere to most.

Archbishop William Temple once remarked, "I'm suspicious of people who are anxious to tell me what God said to them but don't want to hear what God said to me." Sometimes when I get excited about a concern, I tend to be less interested in others' agendas. It's shortsighted of me to think I'm the only one who's hearing from God. In short, living out the pastoral role can keep me honest — it doesn't let me run off on a selfish tangent.

● *It keeps the issue in focus.* Being genuine means telling people how I feel about things. But in many instances, sharing my feelings merely sidetracks ministry.

For instance, if the church board is in the midst of a debate and I tell people how I *feel* about the process or the topic being debated — for example, "I feel uncomfortable with the anger being exchanged" or "This topic troubles me" — I merely shift the subject from the topic under discussion to Pastor Ben's feelings. That undercuts the importance of a matter under discussion and puts off a decision even longer.

● *It keeps emotions in control.* Years ago, when people would treat me badly, I'd get angry and blast them and then try to justify the emotional outburst, muttering things like "righteous indignation," "justice," and "honesty." But the truth was I only hurt the person by satisfying my desire to get even.

The pastoral role, however, can keep such things from happening — protecting me, and others from me. The role helps me realize there is more at stake than my honesty.

Sometimes, of course, even when I'm in the pastoral role, I'll tell another, "I'm mad at you," or "You've hurt me." But first I've asked myself, *Is what I want to say edifying to this person? Does it build up? What is God's desire for him or her at this time?*

● *It enables me to love when I don't feel like it.* Some afternoons I have a series of back-to-back counseling sessions. After one session in which I will have listened to someone in great distress, I'll begin another, yet all the emotions of the previous session are still reeling inside me, making it hard to concentrate.

At such moments, raw authenticity would cause me to say, "Listen, I can't listen to you right now. I'm hurt and concerned about someone who's just been in here." In extreme situations, I might do just that. But most of the time, ministry is furthered if I fulfill my role, putting a smile on my face, nodding at the person's concerns, and giving myself to the one who has come to see me.

• *It focuses the attention on Jesus Christ.* Playing the pastoral role points me to something greater than me. John the Baptist said, "I must decrease; he must increase." That statement should be my goal in every facet of ministry. My preaching should focus on Christ, not on authentic sharing of myself. I don't want people to say, "Wow, what a neat guy" but "I see Christ glorified in him."

When I lead the liturgy, I don't want to be an emcee or entertainer, drawing attention to my wittiness or personality but one who draws people's attention to what is being said in the liturgy: Jesus Christ is Lord.

In short, if I'm only interested in my authentic self or my feelings, the message is lost; people think more about Ben Patterson and less about the gospel.

Beyond Role Playing

One of the longest nights of my life took place at a wedding rehearsal dinner. I felt the guests, none of whom had I met before, were either mildly belligerent or even hostile to me. It was awful. But my pastoral role demanded I be pleasant.

Still, I felt as if I were skimming through a mental card catalog, pulling out random topics to talk about: "Well, how about them Giants?" and "Do you believe this rain!" Someone finally would respond, and another long silence would follow. I was glad when it came time to eat; at least it gave me something easy to do.

Fortunately, not all of ministry has to be so endured. Sometimes it's better to step out of the role and be myself. In fact, I've found five advantages to being genuine in ministry.

• *It helps people — and me — accept my limitations.* Every pastor has limitations, and we shouldn't have to hide them, pretending that we fit perfectly into every pastoral role.

For instance, my predecessor in this church was in many ways my opposite. A marvelous pastor, he got jazzed when he was around people; he served as honorary chaplain of the fire and police departments and borough council. He was at home in a crowd.

That role, though, has always intimidated me. I don't like being the community chaplain — cutting the ribbons, speaking at parades, keynoting the anniversary celebrations. I realize these occasions can be important, that chitchat builds bridges, but all that still tires me.

It's been a great relief to acknowledge publicly that I am an introvert, that I get physically weary from being around large groups of people for long, and that there's nothing wrong with me when I do.

I recognize that in order to fulfill my pastoral responsibilities, I have to be in many such settings. But I don't have to agonize about my discomfort or doubt my calling. It's one part of ministry I'll never be comfortable with.

Sharing that fact can also help my congregation understand when I don't get as involved in community affairs as did my predecessor, and when I don't come off as well when I do.

● *It short-circuits loneliness.* I hate going to presbytery, the bimonthly gathering of pastors and elders of local Presbyterian congregations. It's such a lonely time. Everybody's in their role, especially the pastors. We're a competitive lot, and it's hard to let our guards down.

I can't perform ministry that way. If I keep my feelings inside all the time, then I isolate myself from the Christian community. It's only when I express what's in my heart that people draw closer to me.

For me, it's especially important that I feel at home in my church. If I can't mess up or say what I think about things there, then I become isolated in my role.

● *It keeps ministry moving.* The stress of a board member's day can easily interfere with the business of the board meeting at night. The issue in question can become an occasion to work out the fight someone had with their wife or the lousy day another had at the office.

Before every board meeting, then, we spend an hour in worship, sharing, and prayer. When I participate in this time, it breaks down the pastoral persona so that others feel more free to let down their various personas. That allows us to deal with the hurts and frustrations we've experienced during the week. The result: when we deal with the business of the church, we deal with only that and so finish our business a lot faster.

• *People encounter a real gospel.* People are much more interesting than any function they serve. I can play a role and even play a crowd, but I will not connect with people if I do. It's only when I reveal my humanity, confessing some of my faults and weaknesses publicly, that people relate to me.

And then they can relate better to the gospel. When people see my humanity and the gospel as a vital part of their pastor's life, they're more likely to think Christ can be a vital part of their lives, too.

"The Word became flesh." The Word became a real human being; he didn't just play the role of a human being (that in fact was an early heresy). And it was as a human being that he connected with people.

Pulpit Discretion — The Better Part of Honesty

The line, then, between the pastoral persona and who we genuinely are may never be as clear and distinct as we'd like. However, when I find myself consistently on one side of that line, something is wrong. It's not one or the other — I must incorporate both.

How and when I do that is another matter. In fact, each area of ministry — counseling, administration, community chaplain — requires a separate discussion. Let me here suggest how I handle the performance factor from the pulpit.

As much as I believe in saying what's on my heart and mind, only some things are appropriate for a pastor to share from the pulpit. Here is how I handle sensitive areas with care.

● *Discouragement.* I don't publicly admit I am discouraged when I am discouraged. Although I might tell a close friend, I wouldn't say to my people, "I'm really down. I don't know if I'm going to make it."

I believe that in becoming leaders, we give up our right to be publicly discouraged. Being a leader means being up, positive, and definite. When we announce that we aren't, it can have a devastating effect on our people. They begin to wonder and worry. They begin to lose confidence in the future.

It's important, though, for people to realize that we're not constantly up; otherwise they may wonder if we're all there, if life really affects us. So I share discouragement, but only after the fact: "During our building program five years ago, there were many moments when I didn't feel we'd find the money to keep building."

● *Lust.* In front of men's groups, I've admitted feeling lustful. It's something that men struggle with, so when a pastor mentions he is tempted by it but in Christ struggles against it, the reality of the gospel comes through strong.

I don't, however, admit to such before a mixed crowd. It would send the wrong signals. It may, for instance, make some women wonder if I've been thinking about them sexually. That would only get in the way of our pastoral relationship.

But even with men, I've learned to check my confessions of lust. I used to be very transparent. But when I did that, I subtly and inadvertently communicated that lust wasn't so much wrong as it was "natural," in effect, acceptable.

Now I try to share such weaknesses only to the point that it will show others I too struggle, but I don't share so much that giving in to temptation sounds okay.

● *Anger.* It's not appropriate to get angry in the pulpit unless it's clear that my anger is focused outside the congregation, and even then on something relatively abstract, like sin or injustice or the pornography industry. I've not seen many instances when anger directed at my congregation has done much good. Further, declaring my anger at prominent individuals or institutions respected by my people only puts my people on the defensive.

I can, however, talk about my own struggles with anger. In fact, I did that in a sermon some time ago. I told the congregation, "I am an angry man, and I haven't licked it yet. Some of you may not have a handle on it either." I got more response from that sermon than anything I had preached in a long time.

I didn't find it an easy subject to talk about, but it's a topic people want to hear about, because it's something they are anxious to control.

• *Ambition, pride, competitiveness.* In our culture, these are socially acceptable faults. We may formally acknowledge them as wrong, but we secretly admire people who give in to such temptations, because these people are usually "successful."

The danger for me, then, is acknowledging these faults yet using them as a means to brag subtly. When I do admit them, then, I don't candy coat the harm they do to me or others.

• *Failure.* As a leader, I can't go around admitting every little administrative blunder. But if the mistake is big, and if everyone knows it's a mistake, I've got to admit it, at the time it happens or soon after.

When at Irvine, California, I was looking over the worship attendance numbers and, feeling ambitious, decided to recommend to the board that we increase our Sunday morning services to three. I presented my case, twisted a few arms, and finally convinced the board.

But I hadn't done my homework. The numbers were wrong, and my growth projections were a couple years premature. Within a couple of months of trying the new schedule, the strain was becoming apparent — it was difficult to find people to do all the things necessary to pull off each worship service — ushers, greeters, lay readers, and so on. It was especially hard on our choir, who found themselves shuttling through more services than they cared for.

I went to a dear friend in the church and said, "Bob, I made a mistake."

He laughed and said, more quickly than I would have liked,

"You really did." With that confirmation in hand, I went to the board and told them I was wrong, and I admitted that it was all my fault.

I could have let the board take the rap since they gave me the go ahead, but it ate at me. It was my information and vision, not theirs.

Some say we shouldn't talk about our failures unless they are moral ones, and even then only discreetly. They argue that people who really need to know we failed probably already do. The best move is to make steps to correct the problem.

I don't agree. If we're going to announce our successes, we should be willing to admit when we've made a big mistake. Nothing can hurt a pastor's credibility more than an inability to admit he or she is wrong. It's nice to always be right, but it's not reality.

Depending on one's personality and the nature of the church we serve, the tension between living out the pastoral role and being genuine will be played out differently. But for me, the decision hinges on the answer to this question: Which will better enhance the ministry of Christ in the church? When I seek to answer that question, my reservations about playing the role and my enthusiasm for authenticity pale, and the glory of Christ better shines.

Strengths alone do not a ministry make.
— Kent Hughes

CHAPTER SIX
Working With My Weaknesses

Soon after I became a Christian in high school, I was certain God wanted me to preach. But I had a problem: shyness. Even today, when I'm with new acquaintances, I'm not the type to assert myself. I'm perfectly happy to sit at the back and follow other people's lead.

Since I had been called to preach, though, I knew I would have to deal with this weakness. So as a teenager, I intentionally took leadership positions, responsibilities that would put me in front of people. I was a student body officer in high school and a leader in my church youth group.

In front of such groups, I was terrified the whole time. At times I achieved the illusion of being a confident, articulate leader, but I wasn't. Nothing I did was spontaneous. Even with announcements, I'd prepare a script so that I wouldn't mess up.

As a seminarian, I remained nervous when up front. When I led devotions, I made sure not to look at my wife, because if I caught her eye I would be distracted by concern over how I was doing. At times I'd get twitches in my cheek, my eyes would water, and I'd blush.

Yet I still felt called to public ministry. Today people tell me I'm an accomplished preacher, and I've been a pastor so long they think I naturally fit the role. Many in my congregation would never suspect my basic shyness.

All this convinces me that pastoral ministry means more than using one's strengths for Christ. In fact, I've come to believe that Christ uses our weaknesses in ministry as much as our strengths.

Some people wonder, *Isn't it poor stewardship of one's time and energy to work on a weakness? Doesn't God create us with strengths so we can major on them, and by doing so, work most efficiently and fruitfully for him?*

Others think, *Doesn't God want us to enjoy ministry? And won't we receive the most joy in ministry when we go with our strengths, things we naturally do well?*

These questions reflect a kernel of truth, of course. But over my twenty-three years of ministry, I've found that strengths are only part of the pastoral picture. To be an effective pastor, I've had to work out of my weaknesses, too. Here's what I've noticed along the way.

Strengths Are Not Omnipotent

It's fun to work in areas of strength. I find ministry less toilsome and more enjoyable when I do. But I've also noticed strengths have a downside.

● *Overconfidence.* I've seen many gifted high school athletes. They quarterback the football team, pitch and hit superbly in baseball, or score high in basketball. Then they go to college, and I never hear of them again.

Often I've later discovered that the gifted young athlete had become uncoachable. He was so confident in his abilities, he didn't relish advice or practice. Soon he was passed by less gifted but more coachable athletes.

I've also known some gifted preachers who didn't go far. It was apparent that even in seminary they knew how to use language. Their timing was superb, and there was a magnetism about their physique and bearing.

But because they met so much early success, they stopped honing their preaching skills. They stopped studying. They wouldn't take seriously others' comments. Instead of relying on the Lord in prayer and working hard, they began to rely on clichés and technique. They calcified. Giftedness doesn't last without effort.

● *Self-reliance.* We don't have as much problem giving our weaknesses to God. Since we don't think we have much choice, it's easy to tell God, "I'm not good in administration. Lord, help me."

The problem is giving him our strengths. Oswald Chambers says,

> God can achieve his purpose either through the absence of human power and resources, or the abandonment of reliance on them. All through history God has chosen and used nobodies, because the unusual dependence on him made possible the unique display of his power and grace. He chose and used somebodies only when they renounced dependence on their natural abilities and resources.

Of course, God has also chosen to use people with great gifts — Augustine and his intellect, Spurgeon and his eloquence — but only when they renounced dependence on their natural abilities and resources.

But strengths don't lend themselves to such humility. In some ways, they make godly ministry more difficult.

● *Strengths are not gifts.* Up to this point I've used *strengths* and *gifts* as synonyms. Ultimately I know they are not. Some people are strong communicators but not gifted by the Spirit to preach. Others are efficient administrators, but they don't have the gift of godly administration.

The difference is simply this: A strength is something we do well or easily and enjoy doing. A gift is a skill, strong or weak, that God uses for bearing spiritual fruit.

I'm a good administrator, but I'm not naturally gifted in or motivated to do administration. I don't find it enjoyable. The constant drudgery of the task makes it difficult to face.

However, the daily discipline of intelligently attacking a task I naturally dislike has made me a competent administrator. In fact, my staff says I run a "tight ship," and by God's grace, lives have been blessed. I've overseen programs and guided staff people well enough to minister indirectly to others — many more than I could have through my direct contact.

But if early on I had determined that because of my lack of interest in administration I shouldn't spend much time at it, I would have missed this God-given opportunity to minister.

● *Procrastination, personal and corporate.* I often hear that a church should wait for the gifted, meaning those with natural talent, to come forth before it undertakes a ministry.

Again, there's a measure of truth in that logic, but it can be turned the wrong way: if such-and-such isn't my gift, then I have no responsibility to get involved. I've been in too many situations, however, where waiting for talented people to come forth led to procrastination of obedience to Christ.

But there are too many needful things to be done to wait around for someone to feel gifted. In fact, I've noticed that when some things need doing — like cleaning up after Sunday school or doing dishes after a church dinner or putting away chairs or repainting the choir room — there is an acute shortage of people who feel gifted! Nonetheless such things need to get done.

Strengths alone, then, do not a ministry make.

Needs First, Strengths Second

To put all this positively: I've found it much more helpful first to determine not my strengths but rather the areas of greatest need in the church and community. When I do that, I've noticed that much more of Christ's work gets done.

The most obvious case in point is the need for people to hear about Christ. Evangelism has never come easily for me. But in each of my ministry settings, I've made it a point to evangelize and to train others to do it.

When I was a youth pastor, I'd take my kids with me when I would preach on the streets. Such preaching was hard for me, but I knew I was called to do it.

In my last church, I taught Evangelism Explosion and then regularly went calling with people. In homes I would sit, sometimes so nervous I'd be sick to my stomach, and talk to people about their souls.

In both cases, evangelism needed to be done. I didn't feel I could wait until people who thought they had the gift of evangelism came along to lead us. I was the pastor, so I was responsible for leading in evangelism.

Now if it's not my strength, I may not make a life-time commitment to train people in Evangelism Explosion. But strength or not, I may have to commit three, four, or five years of time and energy to get the ministry started.

In this context, I often think of Mother Theresa. I doubt if she thinks of herself as gifted at changing bedpans. I doubt she finds that fun, but she's called to meet the needs of the dying, so she does what needs to be done.

Ministry is like war and ministers like platoon leaders. Sometimes platoon leaders give orders; sometimes they fire on the enemy; sometimes they clear minefields; sometimes they carry the wounded; sometimes they bolster the frightened with horse play.

Platoon leaders don't spend a lot of time deciding if they're talented at shooting or good at carrying the wounded or gifted at finding mines. Likewise, when you're fighting principalities and powers in high places, it's usually more productive for the kingdom to do things that need doing when they need doing, regardless of one's strengths.

The Renaissance Pastor

Almost all pastors have to give leadership in more areas than they can possibly have strengths. To be an effective pastor, then, I must be a Renaissance pastor.

I have to be an administrator, managing well the life and business of the church; a communicator, teaching my people the good news; a visionary, leading people to new vistas; a contemplative, listening to the voice of God; a compassionate person, hearing the hurts of people; a decision maker, making the many hard choices of church life.

If I were to concentrate my ministry in one or two areas of strength, I think my ministry would become flat. For example, I've known ministers who think of themselves as primarily communicators. The problem is, when they are away from a pulpit or lectern, they are not very interesting people. They are even less effective pastors.

Because ministry for me is an occupation that demands my attention in many areas, it stretches me — about as much as I can be stretched!

In addition, I've found that working on one skill often improves another. For example, I wouldn't say I have the gift of mercy. I don't enjoy, as some do, going from room to room in a hospital, ministering to the ill. But I regularly do hospital visitation, though I could easily delegate the entire task to the rest of my staff.

And I've never regretted going. First, I get to know my people. And second, by knowing my people, I've become a better preacher, one who can connect with their real struggles.

A Renaissance pastor is not only a more interesting person, but a better pastor.

Strengthening Weaknesses

If needs come before strengths for the Renaissance pastor, it means weaknesses need to be attended to. But how do we improve our inadequacies? Here's what I've done.

• *Solicit honest feedback.* A turning point in my ministry occurred one Sunday afternoon when I was in my early thirties. I wasn't feeling good about my sermon. So I asked my wife, "What did you think of the sermon?"

Well, she began to tell me, and I didn't like what I was hearing. So I started arguing with her.

She was small of stature but forceful in her response: "If you want my opinion, don't argue with me when I give it. If you don't want it, please don't ask me."

I was steamed. It took me half a week to come to grips with what she said. I finally told her I did indeed want her feedback. Since then my wife tells me the absolute truth, both good and bad, about how I do in the pulpit and in the ministry. By God's grace she's not a critical person, and we know not to discuss the bad report when I'm already feeling down!

But her honest feedback has remarkably improved my ministry, especially my preaching. Consequently, I've expanded my feedback pool over the years. Our staff now evaluates weekly the Sunday morning service. I encourage new staff members to question why we do what we do in the service so we won't fall into empty worship routines. And I try to foster an atmosphere where we can freely say when we think an idea won't work. Sometimes the atmosphere gets thick with disagreement, but that's okay.

On occasion I also solicit feedback from my staff about the sermon. I know they are careful about what they say, so I have to read more between the lines, but they too have helped me learn and grow.

Getting feedback isn't always pleasant, especially when I'm seeking to improve a weakness — after all, it's going to be weak, especially at the beginning of the process. But it's never going to improve if I don't know the truth.

• *Delegate and train.* I'm not a funny person. I don't know how to make people laugh spontaneously, which may explain why I like zany people and comedians like John Cleese. (Maybe I'm gifted at laughing.)

Well, I was a youth pastor for nine years, and if you can't do funny things with a banana, there's little hope for you in youth ministry. So what did I do?

I began developing some of the high schoolers who were funny. I'd also find other adults who could do the zany stuff well and simply delegate that part of the meeting.

Naturally, there were many other factors in the success of my youth ministry, but if we hadn't been able to make youth laugh part of the night, I don't think ninety to one hundred kids would have kept coming every Wednesday night for years.

• *Use strong resources.* Today entertainment so pervades our culture, sermons must not only be interesting but captivating. Consequently, stories and humor are essential. At a minimum, they keep people interested, and at their best, they drive home serious points.

But I'm not a natural story teller. So I compensate by drawing on strong resources — that is, material that is genuinely engaging.

After I was in youth ministry for about five years, I began receiving invitations to speak at youth conferences. That didn't happen because I had suddenly been transformed into a funny person; I had simply learned to make use of good material. I used to tell the story about Jonah getting spit out on the seashore, and I'd tie in the kids' beach experiences (getting greased up with cocoa butter, having sand stick to your body), and allude to Jonah's likely aroma, texture, and appearance. No wonder people repented! Not a lot of that shtick was original — most of it was material I'd heard here and there and pieced together. But it worked to make youth groups laugh.

For my sermons, I memorize good stories, knowing that otherwise I'll forget key parts. In fact, if you ask me to relate the humor or story I told in a sermon from two days earlier, I can't remember it. But, when practiced for timing and delivery stories work beautifully in a sermon when the material itself is good.

• *Deal quickly with what you hate.* I hate confronting people. While some people thrive on that sort of encounter, exhortation is plainly not my strength. Nonetheless, when I must confront, I find it best to attend to the matter as soon as possible. If I procrastinate, the situation only becomes worse, and since I'm not particularly gifted at it, the encounter also becomes worse.

A couple of times in the past I've delayed confronting staff members who weren't performing well. For instance, once I failed to convey adequately to a staff person the intensity of what was being said about him — how much people were dissatisfied with his inability to follow through on assignments.

Because I let my dislike for confrontation dictate relative inaction, it became worse for everybody. A little dissatisfaction slowly grew into a mushroom cloud of frustration for many people — members became more angry, and I finally had to let the staff member go —which was utterly distasteful to me.

Had I confronted my colleague with more specifics, he would have had a chance to improve or bow out before the situation became so painful. Not only that, our relationship would not have undergone increasing strain.

Now when a small concern presents itself, I immediately see the person in question. That way little things don't build and become even harder to deal with.

• *Practice makes much better.* If a man of moderate athletic ability shot five hundred free throws every lunch hour, he'd get better at free throws. If he hired a coach to critique his technique, he'd get even better. Because this hypothetical man is not particularly gifted, he will never be as proficient as Larry Bird, but he'll be very good.

I know lots of pastors who are effective communicators. They're not particularly gifted — not in the same league as Billy Graham or Chuck Swindoll—but they have exercised a profound dependence on God. In addition, they've asked for critiques of their preaching; they've written out their sermons to avoid clichés; they've memorized their transitions; they've attended preaching clinics. As a result, they're able to engage their listeners and drive home the Christian message.

Practice may never make us perfect, but it certainly makes us much, much better.

Certainly there is a place to talk about the effective use of our God-given strengths. But in my ministry, it's been equally vital to work on my weaknesses. When Paul talked about God using our weakness, I'm sure he meant that in our weaknesses we tend to depend more on God, allowing God to work more through us. Without denying that, I would also add that by God's grace, our weaknesses can be improved and be used effectively by him.

The line between legitimate and illegitimate accountability is sometimes blurry. Nonetheless, it does us well to try to determine when that line has been crossed.

— *Paul Cedar*

CHAPTER SEVEN
Accountability That Makes Sense

Several years ago, I pastored a church that became involved in a dispute initiated by one of our neighbors. We thought the neighbor both unreasonable and inaccurate in his charges. And if we acceded to his wishes, it was going to cost us a great deal of money.

The church's leaders asked me to sit down with him. When I did, I began, "We at the church are grieved to hear we're having these misunderstandings. I can't promise to solve them, but I want to listen and help in every way possible."

After discussing the issue without progress, I finally said,

"Our Lord clearly told us to be good neighbors. Although we think your request is unreasonable, it seems to us that if anyone needs to compromise in this dispute, it's us. Obeying the Lord is more important to us than winning a fight."

Well, you never saw a man's attitude change so quickly. Within two hours we had resolved everything. Sometime later the mayor, whom we had asked to help adjudicate the dispute, called and said, "I don't know what you said or what you did, but this man thinks you're the greatest church on earth."

Not only did we gain favor with this action, we never paid the money that was originally requested. When our relationship became right, our neighbor's attitude became right. What enabled that to happen was the strong sense of accountability the leaders felt toward our community.

Not only are churches accountable to others, but so are pastors. Biblically we are to be accountable to God, to the Christian community, and, in some ways, to civic government and the community in which we minister. The Lord has created us with the need to be accountable to him and to others. When we aren't, we're not only being disobedient to God's Word, we're likely to get ourselves into trouble, even scandal.

So I'm convinced accountability is essential for pastors. Yet a pastor's accountability can be difficult to structure. Sometimes it turns into an excuse for others to complain about the pastor, or worse, to try to control the pastor. When that happens, accountability does more harm than good.

Over the years, I've experienced some of that unhealthy accountability. But most of the time, accountability has been a positive experience, helping me be the pastor and person God desires me to be.

Signs of Illegitimate Accountability

Sometimes we chafe under another's accountability simply because we're prideful. Other times, though, we chafe because we sense something other than loving guidance is being offered. Admittedly, the line between legitimate and illegitimate accountability sometimes becomes blurry. Nonetheless, it does us well to try to determine when that line has been crossed.

Here are four questions I ask that help me determine the legitimacy of the accountability offered me.

• *Are people holding me accountable for their personal expectations?* Because my predecessor arrived at the office at 7:30 each morning, I hear criticism for coming at 8:30. Because the famous television evangelist preaches loudly, while I use measured tones, critics challenge my zeal. Because I visited one member in the hospital every other day instead of daily, word spreads that I don't care about people.

Catering to such expectations takes a tremendous toll, if it doesn't kill us. We cannot meet each person's individual agenda. So, when I sense that someone expects me, in the name of accountability, to meet merely his or her personal expectations, I graciously decline.

In this regard, I found it helpful as a pastor to have a written position description, the summary of which I communicated regularly to the congregation. That kept to a minimum this form of illegitimate accountability.

• *Are people trying to control me?* I once sat in a meeting with some of the past leaders of our church, a group of about six or seven executives, strong personalities, who were upset over how I had handled a recent decision-making process in the church. Having gotten word indirectly of their feelings, I had suggested we meet.

After we gathered, they asked, "Why didn't you come to us for counsel instead of sharing your decision with the whole congregation?"

"Well, guys, not one of you are in office at the present time," I began. "You're not a part of the structure. You're personal friends, and our discussion is certainly appropriate at that level. But you can't set up an ad hoc committee. I'm accountable clearly through our church's structure, and I'm sorry none of you are in that structure right now. If you have concerns, come to me, or come to the people who are in the structure."

• *Are people nit-picking?* Sometimes, when pressure builds, people exaggerate our mistakes and weak points. I may have preached a dozen life-changing sermons but botched the planning of one fellowship event. A pastor may have been gracious in five thousand situations but testy in one late-night phone call. But it's the mistake that people tend to focus on. It may be that people dislike what we're doing, so they latch on to the one mistake to justify strong opposition.

• *Do people have a critical spirit?* Some time ago, I met with a church board unhappy with their pastor, a gifted young man. After discussing the reasons for their discontent, I finally asked, "What are you doing to help him mature in the areas where he lacks? How are you ministering to him? Is he aware of these problems? Have you talked to him about them?"

These questions completely surprised them. They had never considered they had a responsibility to build up that young man.

In short, fruitful accountability — versus mere criticism — is constructive rather than destructive, edifying rather than selfish. There must be a motivation to advance the kingdom of God and to build the life of the person who's being held accountable.

Spheres of Accountability

All these types of illegitimate accountability have one thing in common: people assume that the pastor's ministry revolves around their concerns. That is an oppressive assumption to live under.

So in order to prevent one sphere of my ministry, or one person's perspective, from dominating the whole, I find it helpful to remember that I'm accountable in a number of areas. Sometimes, for instance, the demands of the church seem justified, until I consider my responsibilities to be a good father and husband.

So knowing my spheres of accountability — for me there are six — helps me determine where and when I should be legitimately guided by others.

• *To God.* To the Lord we owe ultimate allegiance. We faithfully answer to others only because we are trying to please him. Even though others may sometimes be dissatisfied with us, which is inevitable, if we aim to please the Lord, we are on the right track in terms of accountability.

Basically, being accountable to God means obedience and faith. The people who have embodied faith, whether Abraham or the entire roll call of Hebrews 11, simply obeyed when God commanded. That simple act of obedience is the essence of biblical faith and biblical accountability.

For me, knowing when and how to obey begins in maintaining a strong devotional time with God. I am ever aware that even while getting straight A's from people, I can flunk with God. Thus I consider my "quiet time" my first priority each day. Increasingly, I sense the need to spend time alone with the Lord. For example, I try to spend a day a month in prayer and fasting, studying the Word, and just being quiet before him. Such times give me perspective and help me to sort out the varied advice that comes my way and to respond to those who offer me healthy accountability.

● *To the members of the body.* I am accountable to the church for a number of things: leadership, pastoral care, administration, modeling the Christian life, to name a few. But above all, I feel I have a responsibility to feed God's flock and nurture his people. That means I have to give myself to serious study, in preparation for teaching and preaching.

That's not easy for me. I'm a people person. I'd much rather spend time being with my people, giving formal and informal pastoral care. But my people need something more from me.

Consequently, I have recruited others to check on me periodically. Recently, when I saw Ted Engstrom, the first thing he asked was "How's your study time?" Knowing he and others will be kind enough to ask that simple question helps me stay in the study when I should.

● *To local church leaders.* They need my leadership, my vision, and my direction. I'm the point man in defining our philosophy of ministry, mission statement, and goals, both short term and long. No one else can do this for the church.

I choose to be accountable to our leaders, also, in the conduct of my personal and professional life. Specifically, this includes living up to the elder's qualifications in 1 and 2 Timothy and Titus as well as the specific areas outlined in my position description.

When leaders sense a shortfall in me and ask, "Could this be a problem?" I respond appreciatively. Sometimes, of course, it hurts to hear such input, but when the concern is shared with a humble and caring spirit, I can respond appropriately.

• *To my family.* Accountability with my family begins with my taking a weekly Sabbath. For many years I did not take a regular day off, nor did my wife Jeannie. But the time came when we felt we should begin doing so, first because the Lord commands his people to take a regular Sabbath, and second because we felt our ministry, our family, and the church would be enhanced and enriched. Having Jeannie work with me on it has made me more consistent about taking a weekly Sabbath.

I've also found it helpful to ask my family to hold me accountable for my ministry.

For instance, before I married Jeannie, I knew I was called to a ministry of evangelism. She understood that we might have to live an itinerant life. Still, I told her, "Jeannie, as I commit my life to God and to you, I want to promise you something. Whenever I sense the Lord calling me to a ministry, I'll never make the decision alone. I'll be accountable to God and to you. If I sense God saying yes but you sense him saying no, we won't move. We will not budge without unity of heart."

Including my family like this has prevented me from feeling so alone during crucial decisions. Instead, the support and feedback I receive from them encourages me and helps me discern God's leading.

• *To the larger church.* When I resigned from Hollywood Presbyterian Church to assume the senior pastorate of Lake Avenue, the most difficult part of the decision was leaving the Presbyterian denomination, to which I had given significant time, energy, and allegiance. I liked being in a connectional system, where at least at an administrative level, ministers and churches were accountable to one another.

Now I'm president of a denomination that practices congregational polity, a polity that also has many strengths. Nonetheless, I want to help our churches and pastors have a sense of accountability one for another. I also want our pastors to feel a sense of responsibility for the larger body of Christ in their community and around their world.

In my opinion, one of the major challenges we face is the Lone Ranger syndrome. Unfortunately, I've seen many pastors who believe they're accountable to no one but themselves, who act as if they are "in charge" of their ministry. That attitude invariably leads to conflicts, divisions, and resentments, not only within their ministries but also without.

At one recent evangelism seminar, for instance, a Methodist pastor approached me, and after we had talked awhile, he apologetically said, "I've got a problem that I hate to tell you about. In our city, one pastor from your denomination acts like a separatist. He's unwilling to cooperate with pastors of some other denominations. In fact, the pastor is divisive in many ways."

"Don't apologize for sharing that information with me," I responded. "That's the kind of thing I want to know. In my opinion, such pastors are out of line and need to be called to accountability. That conduct not only denies the spirit and charter of this denomination, it denies the Spirit of Christ and his prayer for unity."

So, whatever position I've been in, I've always given some of my time and energy to promoting cooperation among churches.

• *To the community.* When we were starting a building program at one church I served, we saw we were beginning with a handicap: several area churches were feuding with the city. It was front page news. It spooked several of our building committee people, who were leery about getting permits from local government agencies.

So I took a couple of key people from the church, and we met with the mayor, then the city manager, then with people from the building permit office, telling each of them: "We are privileged to be a part of our city. We want you to know we do not expect any special favors. We will follow the rules and guidelines you've established. We know that you want to protect the integrity and beauty of the city. Please know that we will do whatever we have to do to cooperate with you."

Afterward those city leaders were responsive, excited, and appreciative. In fact, the mayor and city council people would in public meetings compliment us, thanking the church for the way we worked with the city.

Because of the command to render to Caesar the things that are Caesar's, pastors, as leaders of local churches, need to be accountable to the local authorities, at least as long as it doesn't compromise the integrity of the gospel.

As I mentioned, knowing I have responsibilities in each of these spheres prevents people in one sphere from trying to hold me accountable too strongly in one area. The extended church, for example, can expect some of my time and energy, but not so much that it undermines my ministry to the local church.

Naturally, there will be times when people from different spheres will each make legitimate demands of me. Sometimes my family needs me just at the time the church needs me. Earlier I mentioned an incident in which I wanted to be a good steward of the church's money, yet at the same time I wanted to be a good neighbor.

I try to resolve such conflicts in two ways. First, I spend time in prayer, seeking the Lord and his will. I find that what I should do often becomes clear afterward.

Second, I've found it helpful to have a "kitchen cabinet," which includes past chairpersons of the major church boards. At Lake Avenue, mine included all the men who, during the previous pastoral tenure to the present, had chaired one of the church's boards. I tried to meet with them on a monthly basis to receive their counsel, to bounce ideas off of them, and to pray with them.

How to Foster Legitimate Accountability

In order to foster legitimate accountability, we need to do more than maintain a broad perspective on our responsibilities. We also need to take positive action to encourage helpful and healthy accountability. Here are four ways I've done that.

1. Welcome it. Although it's difficult for me, I try not to be defensive when someone offers me a suggestion. I try to maintain an open ear for feedback and a willingness to honestly evaluate the suggested counsel. If I get tense, everybody gets tense, and that makes accountability all the more difficult.

It's not easy to simply welcome guidance from others. Some people who've known me for years say I'm hypersensitive. Part of that is by choice. A pastor's heart must be acutely sensitive both to hear the Holy Spirit and empathize with people. If I were to protect myself with defense mechanisms, I'd become hard and calloused —that's too steep a price to pay. I think criticism stung Jesus, and so I think it's natural that we wince at pain. As I've matured, though, I'm learning not to overreact.

2. Model it. Holding others accountable requires a willingness to confront others with some difficult truths, and with love. This approach usually resolves the problem while building up the person who's involved.

At the same time, it models to others how they can hold us accountable as leaders. It's a form of the golden rule, of treating others as we would want them to treat us.

On one occasion I was mediating a dispute between two church leaders. Abruptly, one of them made a serious accusation against a third person who was not present. Although the man had shared the accusation with a number of people in the church, he had never followed the biblical injunction to first talk with the person he was accusing.

"My brother," I said, "we cannot go on without talking about this. You've made a serious accusation that questions the reputation of a highly esteemed leader. Have you gone to him and talked about this?"

He sputtered and stammered. I continued in a gentle but forthright manner. "Biblically and practically speaking, you have sinned against your brother. You need to follow the biblical injunction to go to him, meekly and gently. I encourage you to do that, and I will be happy to help you in any way I can."

3. When confronting, use the opportunity to plainly teach about accountability. I try to talk about what I am doing and why — what principles are guiding my confrontation. I think that was one of the geniuses of Christ's teaching style: he used conflict and misunderstandings as a well lit stage for instruction.

When I confront, I try to say, "The reason I'm going through the discomfort of bringing this to your attention is that I want your best. We all have blind spots, things that hurt us, and if no one loves us enough to tell us about them kindly, we suffer unnecessarily all of our lives. I'm not saying this because I'm angry at you or against you but because I'm for you."

4. Never question people's motives. Accusations are like chemical weapons: they poison the atmosphere. Early in my ministry God taught me a lesson when I was hurt by something a brother in Christ had said and done. Since I had assumed it was his motive to hurt me, I felt a great deal of pain and anger.

Nonetheless, I felt encouraged by the Spirit to go to him to ask why he had done and said such things. Much to my surprise, he said what had happened was unintentional and that his motive had not been malicious.

God used that occasion to help me make an important commitment early in my ministry, that is, that I would never question another person's motives. So now, when I wonder what's driving others, instead of jumping to conclusions, I try to go to them. In lieu of accusing, I say something such as, "I may be wrong, but it looks to me that so-and-so happened. Tell me how you're feeling about it."

In addition to the sense of freedom such a decision can bring us, it also provides a model of how people should respond to us when they feel hurt or confused by something we've said or done. When I refuse to question other's motives, they are less likely to question mine.

I believe that accountability is absolutely essential for all Christians, especially Christian leaders. To obey Christ and follow him as Lord is the heart of true Christian accountability, but being accountable to others at various levels remains vital. When we belong to Christ, we belong to each other. And no member of the body can go it alone.

PART THREE

The Personal Side of Pastoring

In the long run, I contribute to the church most by being a man with a good marriage and a reasonably healthy family.

— Ben Patterson

CHAPTER EIGHT

Balancing Family, Church, and Personal Time

You might call it cruising or hanging out. In my family we call it "oozing": nothing in particular to do, everything in general, whenever we feel like it, if we do. It's the polar opposite of the way the rest of our lives are lived.

Some people complain when they have nothing to do. We rejoice. With G. K. Chesterton, we never have enough of nothing to do. The Pattersons love to ooze. We hoard like hidden treasure those days when we can just watch television, start reading but never finish four or five books and a dozen magazines, walk aimlessly around town, or talk and drink coffee till we're giddy with caffeine.

Recently my wife, Lauretta, went to visit her family in Minnesota for a week. She took along our daughter, Mary, and left the boys and me to fend for ourselves. So, we oozed for the whole week, consuming junk food and renting videos every day. I even cleared my afternoons; every day after school, I welcomed my boys at the door.

The church, however, also anticipated our week of bachelorhood. We received numerous dinner invitations, as the ladies of our church looked to mother us with their chicken dinners. It was a wonderful gesture; I guess they thought we'd starve. But microwaved burritos and pepperoni pizza sounded just fine to us. So as tactfully as I could, I refused their generosity, explaining vaguely that we had other plans — plans to ooze with the guys!

Juggling church, family, and personal time is a nagging source of tension for pastors. Our culture organizes around the weekend, but weekends for the minister are work days. On top of that, our weekdays don't end at five o'clock. So the lines between ministry and family time are constantly crossed.

I often come to the end of my week feeling like a quarter miler gasping for breath at the end of a race. The debt is not for oxygen in my body but for oxygen in my soul: ooze time with the ones I love. And as an introvert I feel acutely the crunch on my alone time. There are times when ministry seems interminable.

Over the years, though, I've made some progress at keeping these areas in balance. Here are some insights that help me do that.

Know Your Signals of Imbalance

Balancing these areas begins with reading the signals of overload. We all have them.

For instance, the bathroom scale often tips me off. I envy the people who, under stress, lose their appetite. For me, though, it's just the opposite. Weight gain is a good indicator that I'm under stress and that my life is out of control.

Anger is another signal. Sudden explosions toward my

family broadcast to me that I'm under pressure.

Still another is when the kids start resenting my instructions. If my discipline is reasonable, and they become annoyed with me anyway, that's a clue my family misses their dad.

Feeling that my family is just another thing I have to do is another yellow light. When I am so tired and harassed that I approach what ought to be ooze time as a chore, I know something has gone wrong.

So, when one or more of these signals get my attention, I know it's time to put my life in better balance.

Keep the Sabbath Free from Necessity

More than anything else, for me a healthy and balanced life is the product of keeping a regular Sabbath. By stopping for a day, the Sabbath sets every activity and responsibility back in its proper place.

My childhood Sundays were consumed with nonstop church meetings. As a youth minister and pastor, I kept up that wearying tradition. Imagine my surprise and delight, then, upon discovering a Jewish rabbi, Abraham Heschel, who actually felt thrilled about the Sabbath. His book, *The Sabbath*, is about a love affair with the seventh day. To Heschel, it is a gift to cherish, a joy to be anticipated rather than a day to endure.

For pastors, a day off during the week is typically packed with domestic obligations. In the early years of our marriage, my day off consisted of "to do" lists — mowing the lawn, running errands, or changing the oil. It didn't feel like Heschel's delightful Sabbath, a season of refreshment and joy.

But once a week, pastors need a Sabbath, a day free from necessity. Today, the Patterson rule of thumb is "If it needs to be done, don't." Whatever day it is, the Sabbath must be rid of all household chores and "to do" lists.

Lauretta and I both became convinced we needed a day where we stopped everything. So we suspended our obsession to produce for one day a week, transforming our days off into seasons of refreshment with our Lord.

Mondays are now occasions for feeding our souls. An open-ended day allows for a fresh anticipation of God. Our Sabbath actually starts, however, on Sunday evening, similar to the Jewish notion of sundown to sundown. We usually hang out all evening, making popcorn and viewing the tube. We don't even urge the kids to study. By Sunday evening, the season for homework is past.

Many of our Sabbath mornings start by eating out for break-fast, and we often combine it with a long walk outdoors. Escaping from the house distracts our minds from the "to do" lists; it allows us to reconnect with each other and with God. The temptation to violate our Sabbaths with busyness, however, is always enticing. But now, whenever I am so tempted, I take an aspirin and lay down until it goes away.

A Sabbath free from necessity, though, brought a new tension into our marriage. Lauretta began saying, "Well, when are you going to mow the lawn?" So we shuffled the lists to other time slots, cramming the lawn mowing, errand running, and oil changing into the other six days. Frankly, though, some things just don't get done now. And that's okay — much of the time.

A routine Sabbath is the quickest exit off the fast lane. In my opinion, Sabbaths and balance are inseparable. By stopping for one day a week, our lives rejuvenate, reconnecting family ties and titil-lating our desire for God once again.

Choosing Activities That Refresh

Lauretta calls it a moral and spiritual blind spot: my taste in movies hovers somewhere around Homer Simpson and Archie Bunker. I like macho movies. I'll take Arnold Schwarzenegger and Danny Glover over Kathryn Hepburn and Laurence Olivier any-time. And when I hunker down with a bag of popcorn and the unambiguous world of a Schwarzenegger video, my world be-comes tolerable again. For me, leading a balanced life demands that I embrace activities that refresh me. And watching Arnold hammer the bad guys while tossing out silly quips in heavy Austrian accents sweeps out the cob webs, letting me escape for a while.

Exercise is also an upper. I usually work weights several times a week and jog as my knee allows. Walking and running really nourish my soul; they're almost like a spiritual discipline; it's alone time.

Working out, however, is also a family hobby. A couple times a week, my boys and I pump iron at the YMCA. They love it, but it just about kills me. My goal is to bench press 300 pounds (like my friend Arnold?) before I turn 50, but the old gray stallion just ain't what he used to be.

Reading also revitalizes me. A friend of mine talks about the difference between micro- and macro-preparation. Micro-preparation is the reading done specifically for a sermon or lesson, merely keeping the wolves away from the door. Macro-preparation, on the other hand, is the reading that has no immediate application. Earl Palmer, pastor of First Presbyterian Church in Berkeley, California, calls it offensive reading. (I've discovered, though, that in the long run, the material amassed in macro-reading usually ends up in a sermon or lesson anyway.)

Macro-preparation, whether it's reading novels or watching movies, rounds out both my personal life and ministry. In fact, I measure a good week by whether or not I've been able to give half a day to reading something fun or interesting.

Appreciating Your Limitations

The multitudinous hats worn by the pastor often contribute to the drudgery of ministry. It's simply impossible to do everything well. So part of being a balanced pastor is an astute self-awareness, an appreciation of your limits.

Take church administration. Please. I'm nearly 49 years old and still haven't become the crack manager I imagined in my youth I would one day become if I just read enough books about it and tried a little harder. But I don't mind. I accept what time and experience have demonstrated I manifestly am not. I've said to myself, *Don't lose any sleep or knock yourself out over it; it's just not worth it.* I no longer see myself as administratively handicapped, but rather, "differently empowered." Now if I can just get up the courage to say that to the people in my congregation . . .

I try to concentrate on what I do well. And that unclutters my calendar while maximizing what I do best. One thing that has stuck with me from the administrative books I read in my hopeful youth was a Peter Drucker maxim for the effective executive: we should determine the one or two things that only we can give to the organization, give it, and delegate everything else. That has reinforced my resolve to consolidate my energies into preaching, teaching, and personal discipleship.

It's important that I know not only *what* but *how much* I can do well in a given month. Sometimes, no matter how much I love something, I just have to say no. Speaking engagements are the hardest for me to turn down. I love the challenge of a new audience and the opportunity to significantly impact people for the kingdom. And I also love to write. But permitting only a few of my outside loves helps me keep my equilibrium.

That holds especially true as I juggle my various church responsibilities. After a month at my present church, I published my priorities in a church newsletter: My number one priority is to pray and to study. Other critical ministries like working with the staff and the church board, and developing leadership fall second on my list. And everything else follows as time allows.

The size of our church staff, I realize, grants me that kind of flexibility. But every pastor faces opportunity costs and ultimately has to make the hard choices.

Give the Church the Fruits of a Healthy Life

The fruits of my walk with Christ and my walk with Lauretta and the children are not easily measured or clearly defined. But modeling a balanced life may be the strongest leadership I can give to a church. In the long run, I contribute to the church most by being a man with a good marriage and a reasonably healthy family.

Lauretta and the kids covet my quantity, not quality, time. For the most part, all those time management pointers are worthless.

I know one busy man who regularly scheduled quality time with his family. One evening after dinner, before he headed off to a meeting, he wanted to shoot baskets with his son. When his son seemed hesitant, the father said, "Come on, let's spend some quality time together." The son replied, "Dad, couldn't we sometimes just have some quantity time together?"

I simply have to be with my family, quality or not. The amount of intimacy with my wife or family is directly related to the time spent with them.

So I find that special moments with my family cannot be orchestrated; I must regularly be accessible to them during unscheduled times. Recently, one of my sons interrupted while I was watching the evening news. He just sort of plopped down beside me on the couch and started a dialogue — about sex no less.

That peek into his life was a priceless moment. A thousand years and lifetimes couldn't have programmed it. But had I not been available, the opportunity would have vanished forever.

That's why the oozing routine of the week when Lauretta and Mary visited Minnesota was so wonderful. It allotted me large chunks of uninterrupted time with my boys. (Although, we now try not to be too excited when Lauretta goes away for the weekend — we'd sure hate for her to think we actually preferred microwaved burritos and pizza to chicken dinners.)

That's also why extended vacations are so important to us. In fact, carving out vacation time is as critical as keeping a weekly Sabbath. Our busy schedules create satellite relationships within the family; we encounter one another now and then but only in passing. We lose our relational contact.

Vacations, though, change all that. The car, tent, or whatever throws our family back together — whether we want to or not. The first two days or so of a Patterson vacation can be pretty rough, with the kids snarling at each other for invasions of private space and Lauretta and me snarling at them for snarling. But quickly we re-learn what it means to be a family, making room again for each other's world. Hours of together time on vacations overhaul our entire family system.

Vacationing near our immediate families, like Lauretta's parents in Minnesota, also allows us extra family time. Grandma's tender loving care always alleviates our daily maintenance concerns, freeing up mom and dad for a more relaxing vacation.

Finally, I can't underestimate the value of spending time together in prayer with my wife, although it's taken us years to learn to do it.

Some time ago, a ruptured disc in my spine put me flat on my back for six weeks. Depression settled over me and fear over Lauretta. With two small children and an uncertain recovery, Lauretta and I felt totally helpless.

Up to that juncture, we had never regularly prayed together. I'm not sure why, perhaps because of my own prayerlessness — if I wasn't praying on my own, why should I want to pray with her?

One night, we began praying together for my back. One thing led to another, and our praying spilled over into other areas.

That particular crisis forced both of us to our knees, intertwining our spiritual lives. The pain of those dismal weeks changed us forever, intimately drawing us together with our Lord. And today, our prayer time is one of the most important parts of each day.

For the church, the time spent with my family never reaches the point of diminishing returns. I don't believe it's selfish for wanting more time with Lauretta, my kids, or even myself. I saw a wonderful title on a book, something like, *If You Don't Find Time to Do It Right, When Are You Going to Find Time to Do It Over?* Not only is there no glory in ministry burnout, trashing my family and personal life, it's just not practical.

I have accepted it as a regretable fact of ministry: there will probably always be a dissatisfaction with the balance between job and home. I resonate with the observation of another minister who also feels the pull: "I can feel good about my involvement at the church, or I can feel good about my involvement at home. I don't know if I have ever felt good about both of them at the same time." It's that tension again.

But the Sabbath allows me to place the whole matter, at least weekly, into the hands of a gracious and providential God.

Taking advantage of the perks of ministry is one of the best ways to foster healthy attitudes toward the church and ministry.

— Kent Hughes

CHAPTER NINE
Helping Your Family Enjoy Ministry

We moved to College Church when our oldest daughter, now a missionary, was sixteen. Holly hadn't wanted to come. Understandably she felt robbed of her identity, having been uprooted from her school, the friends she grew up with, and all she knew and loved. Inside she was an angry young girl.

We knew she was angry and discussed it with her, believing it would soon pass. But within her there was a deeper subterranean river of rage that boiled to the surface after a few months. She had huge resentments against me and the church. I may have been "called" — but she wasn't!

Our sweet daughter, who had never had a rebellious day in her life, became secretive and developed some dangerous relationships that threatened to ruin her life. I actually feared that we might lose her.

At one point, in fact, I began to question my own fitness for ministry — if I failed in parenting, how could I presume to pastor the church?

And what was the cause of this misery? My decision to follow what I believed to be God's call to uproot my happy family and move 2,000 miles to a radically different community and church and engage in a particularly demanding pastorate. The stress of attempting to meet the needs of my congregation and be an effective father repeatedly brought me to desperation.

Pressures like this — and many more endemic to the pastoral calling — make ministry homes particularly vulnerable, as horror stories of preachers' kids sadly remind us.

What is the answer? There are, of course, no guarantees. Venture into ministry and you venture into risk. But my wife and I have discovered some attitudes and actions that help the pastor's family appreciate the ministry and love the church.

Overcoming the Preoccupations

Early in ministry my young family suffered from my preoccupation. The demands of ministry distracted me too easily. I simply could not turn it off when I left the church and went home for the evening. I loved my children and enjoyed them, but nonetheless, I would not be all there sometimes. At supper I would converse, smile, chuckle but inwardly chew on ministry concerns.

Ministry worries didn't drive me as much as career goals. I yearned to succeed, to prove I was worth something. It got so bad that Barbara finally told me directly, "You need help. You need counseling."

When you're in the ministry (a patently spiritual occupation) and in your mid-twenties and trying to be a "man of God," that's a humbling thing to hear. But I took her advice and engaged a professional counselor. After a few sessions he said, "Kent, you're trying to earn self-worth through ministry, and the way you approach life, you wouldn't feel good enough even if you became President of the United States!"

He was right. I was hooked to a barometer that went up and down with my youth ministry — and that is a wild ride to say the least! If attendance was up one Sunday or I taught an effective Bible study, I felt great. If attendance dropped or a program lagged, I felt bad. I measured myself by ministry performance, subject to the vicissitudes of the church.

If my behavior had affected only me, that would have been bad enough. But my preoccupations impaired my whole family: Barbara sometimes had a distant, disengaged husband; my kids had a benign, empty, ecclesiastical father.

It has not been easy, but over the years I have worked to overcome this attitude. I now maximize my ministry time and work efficiently so I don't feel guilty about unfinished work when I go home. On a recent New Year's Day, I remembered I had a load of work waiting at the office. But I pushed the thought completely away, reminding myself of my blessed "obligation" to relax with my family, which I wholeheartedly did.

Barbara also helped me focus on my family when I was home. She made our evening meal a sacred family time. When our family was young, we took the phone off the hook so we could converse without interruptions. Barbara and I would ask each other and the kids a hundred questions. We'd find out what had been happening in each of our lives, making each one feel what they were to us: special.

I have also learned to ask myself, "When I'm no longer pastor here, what will be the things that endure?" After all, on the flow of this church's history, I'm just a blip. (I'd like to think I am more than that, but that's it.) Pastors come and go, and the church goes on.

What will endure are my relationships with my wife and children. They will never come and go. That means coming home at five o'clock regularly (there are exceptions, of course!) and with enough energy left to be fully present.

Barbara and I set a goal for ourselves when we were in our twenties: "We're going to be great grandparents," we said. That goal influenced the way we raised our children, because it gave us a long-term perspective. Now we're grandparents, and we love it! If I had a church of 4,000 but unfulfilling relationships with my children or my wife, it would all be ashes to me.

Sorting Through the Expectations

Raising kids is hard enough without any extra pressure. But like many pastoral families, some people expect pastors' children to act better than their own — as if the atmosphere of the parsonage had mystical powers. My well-behaved kids were somehow supposed to validate my ministry. Barbara and I decided, however, we weren't going to let concern for our reputation determine what we would do with our kids.

Some raised their eyebrows when I let my 13-year-old son William Carey be deejay for school dances. He'd wear a fedora and purple tie and think he was really great. Those who didn't approve of rock music wanted my family to abide by their values.

Since Carey wasn't doing anything illegal, immoral, or for that matter, unbiblical, I stuck to my decision. I didn't want my children to grow up feeling they were living in a pastoral strait-jacket. I wanted them to understand that any restrictions I imposed on them arose from my personal convictions, not my vocation.

Later, when Carey was a senior in high school and his soccer team went to the regional playoffs, the team members decided to have their ears pierced and don a team earring. Some churched and unchurched parents objected, but I did not. Again, it was not a moral or biblical issue. As Christians we have to say no to enough things, so Barbara and I decided to say yes to as many things as possible, saving our noes for the truly important things. Today the earring is long gone. But my son's heart is with me.

When our children were small, we were strict; we held the reins close. As they grew older, we wanted them to give the Lord control of their lives, and we realized they couldn't give to the Lord what wasn't theirs. So we gradually gave them the reins to their lives, hoping and praying they would turn them over to the Lord.

We didn't always approve of what they did, and we often told them why. But little by little we increasingly let them make their own choices. They made a lot of mistakes, but they learned. And best, they were given their own chance to give the reins of their lives to the Lord.

I believe that risky but necessary process would have been jeopardized had we allowed some members' expectations to dictate our children's behavior.

Them or Us?

We wanted our children to develop healthy attitudes toward the church. So when I was working, Barbara would never tell the children, "Dad's at church." She would always say, "Dad's at work" — just like everybody else's father. She didn't want them thinking church was taking their dad away from them. If I had to be gone, let work be the reason.

She also accentuated the positive side of ministry. "Aren't we lucky?" she'd say. "So-and-so's dad is a trucker (or a salesman or whatever) and has to be gone so often. Our dad's a pastor, and he can be home to eat dinner with us every night!"

In fact, taking advantage of the perks of ministry is one of the best ways to foster healthy attitudes toward church and ministry.

For instance, one of those perks is access to church facilities, like the church gym. My boys regularly came to me for the gym key and took their friends over to play basketball. But the deacons, properly concerned about kids hurting themselves without adult supervision, decided that no teenagers should use the gym after office hours or when no adult was present.

Here was potential for huge resentment, I felt. So I had some private conversations, made some guarantees, laid some rules out for the boys, and they continued to enjoy their privilege. If I had not gone to bat for them, little resentments against the church could have started to build.

I also tried to take advantage of speaking engagements. On

some I would take one of my children along — it was a great time to be together. On others I was able to arrange trips for my entire family, like the time I exchanged pulpits with a pastor in Boston, and on July fourth weekend no less. That weekend — with accommodations on the Boston Common, fife and drum parades, the booming salutes of muskets, a stroll along the Charles River, John Williams conducting the 1812 Overture with the Boston Pops on the Esplanade, complete with booming howitzers on the Charles — was one of our most memorable family trips. We saw fireworks in Boston because I was a pastor.

Pastors' children also get more positive attention than most, and that we never discouraged. Especially when I did youth or college ministry, my children were always included. During Saturday night college Bible study in our house, for instance, we'd have sixty collegians, and each of our children would be in someone's lap, just basking in the attention.

Another perk I gave my children was open access to me. If after school they stopped by the office, it didn't matter who was with me, my staff let them in to see me. They didn't abuse the privilege, but once in a while they would strut in. It was a small privilege that signaled they mattered to me more than the church.

A few years ago we returned to visit the church where our children spent their childhood. When we pulled up to the front, a flood of memories swept over us. Our boys were surprised to see the courtyard they played in and said, "Our soccer field, it's so small." It was the church's, of course, but they said "ours." We encouraged that sense of ownership. We wanted them to feel they were part of things, that they belonged.

Since we took advantage of such perks of ministry, our children ended up thinking of the church and ministry more as friends of the family.

Juggling Time and Schedule

The pastor's busy schedule can take a toll on the family. "Normal" people unwind on weekends; pastors are getting keyed up. For others, Christmas and Easter are relaxed family times; for us, they're intense work periods. Since I cannot escape such liabilities, I've tried to balance them with one key asset of ministry: I can virtually schedule anything I want. The pastor's schedule may be abnormal, but it's also flexible.

For example, in my early ministry years, I'd visit the grade school once a month and take one of my children out for lunch. In fact, their friends would be jealous because my kids were "so lucky to get out of school!" It was a big deal for my kids — and me.

Barbara also helped me with this. She alerted me well ahead of time so I could put the children's recitals and school programs on my calendar. When my children's programs conflicted with regularly scheduled church board meetings, I would either reschedule the church meeting, attend late, or on infrequent occasions, simply not attend the meeting. Rather than engendering criticism, I more often received affirmation: "I'm glad our pastor has his priorities in order." (Besides, I was happy to learn that the church's leadership could do quite well without my presence!)

I also learned to work my schedule to my family's advantage. For example, when I pastored in California, we would sometimes take the family for an early morning hike in "Wilderness Park," a park in the nearby foothills, and cook breakfast outdoors before we dropped the children off at school. These fondly remembered times interfered with no one's schedule and gave the whole family a great start on the day. Occasionally Barbara and I even took them out of school to go to the beach. (You can't let school stand in the way of an education!)

Other families can do such things on Saturdays, but my schedule allowed me to make those times a little more special.

Processing Criticism

Recently at a holiday gathering, Barbara and I were reminiscing with our children about our early ministry, and to their surprise, we alluded to some difficulties in one of our parishes. "Dad, you're kidding!" they chorused, "We had no idea."

They were incredulous at what they learned: a few prominent families in our congregation had been seduced by a cultish legalism.

They had rules about child discipline, dress styles, women's hair, and even men's beards and mustaches (a mustache was a sure sign that one had sensual problems!). Some even questioned the wearing of polyester and cotton blends (cf. Lev. 19:19).

For months, I had to endure weekly adrenaline-pumping confrontations and some comic opera (what about mixed fabrics? Good grief!), which left both Barbara and me drained and wounded.

Much of Barbara's and my time together was dominated by our concern, and we often privately discussed the problem at great length. But we never shared the details with our children, because we realized that ministry families are especially vulnerable. Children don't have the capacity to understand relational subtleties or the experience to put such wrongs in perspective.

It's not that we acted like pastoral Pollyannas, whitewashing everything, wearing a perpetual Mona Lisa smile. But we did follow three guidelines:

1. Refrain from talking about church problems or people in front of our children. This included not using sarcasm, biting humor, wry smiles, and knowing glances between us at the mention of a sore spot or a troublesome name.

2. Speak lovingly and respectfully of our congregation, even the disordered personalities.

3. When children realize something is wrong (when people leave the church unhappily, for example), talk about it on a level they can understand and without rancor or bitterness.

As our children matured, they were able to keep things in perspective. Then criticism and difficulties were used as times of instruction about how to act in love during a dispute.

Today my children sometimes challenge me. "Dad, I think you need to watch your attitude about those people." Gulp! Nice role reversal!

Not Acting Poor

I guarded my family from other kinds of resentments as well. There were times, for example, when we lived on the economic edge. We had four children in five years — and this before I was 26 (not the way to the "Fortune 500")! No matter how much we struggled, however, we never bemoaned our finances. Our children felt secure even when their parents didn't.

It was important to me that my children not become resentful over petty material things. I didn't want them blaming the church for not paying Dad enough. One Christian leader experienced grinding poverty during his child-rearing years. But all along he said he piously reminded his children that the family was doing without because they were "serving Jesus." He confided to me that this had laid the foundation for his children's later tragic rebellion.

Barbara and I concentrated on making the most of what we had and saved diligently for special purchases or activities. We always made family vacations extra special. We saved as a family so we could have our annual two weeks in a spacious rental on Newport Beach's beautiful Balboa Island. What marvelous memories: "The sea rhythmic in platinum and blue," I write after one trip to San Onofre. "My daughter's hair more radiant than any jeweler's creation."

Also, although we could never dress our kids in the latest labels, we made sure they weren't embarrassed about what they wore to school.

The central question for me is, *How do I view life?* Materialists come in every economic bracket. A poor minister can be caught up by materialism more than a wealthy man. I knew my attitude about finances would affect my kids' attitudes about the church and God. So ultimately I tried to model contentment for them. I wanted them to see we are blessed when we have a lot, and we are also blessed when we do not.

Patience with Kids

As a pastor, I'm geared to work for and expect change. But it's risky to expect too much too soon, especially with my children. I have to remember parenting is a process.

I know one pastor whose son struggled with doubts, almost driving his parents to distraction with his repeated questions:

"What is truth? Who is God?" His parents could have either panicked or believed that God was with their son in the process. They chose to trust. "If you're *seriously* wondering about it," they'd say, calling his bluff, "why don't you try being a Buddhist?"

They told him they were so convinced that Christianity is the only way, they were willing to let their son give it the ultimate test. They believed God was bigger than their son's questions. They knew God was at work in his life, so they loved him and met him where he was. The last I heard, he was still struggling, but the young man was thinking about becoming a missionary!

God has a timetable for each one of us. He's going to work differently in one person than in another. If I panic when my children go through doubts or trouble, I may circumvent the very thing God wants to do in their lives. If I obtrusively try to solve their problems or get them straightened out, I may prevent the mysterious ways of God. Like fruit that needs time to ripen, children need time for God's process in their lives. And I've found tree-ripened fruit tastes best.

A disproportionate number of ministers' children have become accomplished pastors, politicians, writers, educators, doctors, and scientists — people who have contributed much to humanity. They grew in rich soil where issues were discussed and life had a purpose. They saw the dynamics of human relationships.

But it's also true that a disproportionate number of ministry children have achieved infamy. The pastor's home has potential to launch people both ways. Jesse James and James Dobson are both products of a ministry home.

Barbara and I were not super parents. We didn't have all the answers. But we loved our children and did our best. We blundered through many things, but we survived, and through God's grace and faithfulness have four remarkable children.

Several years ago, when the youngest of our children was a senior in high school, I took all our children out to dinner with the purpose of finding out how they felt about growing up in a pastor's home.

"Did you ever wish I'd done something else? That I'd never

been a pastor?" I asked.

They were unanimous: "No. We can't imagine you doing anything else, nor have we ever wanted you to."

They considered themselves privileged to have been raised in a pastor's home. They liked hearing me preach. They appreciated the many people they met through the years. They liked the fun things ministry allowed our family to do. They said they enjoyed being a part of the ministry. Today they love God and his church.

It was a holy moment, and we thanked God.

I've found it isn't enough to be true to myself and God alone. I must go the second mile, not only that others might not be confused but that ministry might effectively continue.

— *Paul Cedar*

CHAPTER TEN

The Extra Mile of Pastoral Integrity

For nearly three decades of ministry I was unaware of anyone ever questioning my integrity. Then it happened without warning.

A member of the pastoral staff of the church I was serving began telling others he was concerned about my lack of integrity. He had suggested his concern to me during one brief encounter, but I was unaware he was speaking so freely to others.

Then came the day of a church board meeting where we were discussing a serious and potentially divisive matter. When I asked for an open discussion to let board members express their concerns,

I was surprised to find the conversation turn toward me. Three of the board members said that the church's real problem was not the issue under discussion but me. They said they had questions about my personal integrity.

I was shocked. In disbelief, I asked them what they were especially concerned about, but they were vague. As we proceeded, I figured out that the common denominator of their concern was their respect for one of the other pastoral staff who had sowed seeds of suspicion about me in their minds.

Unfortunately, this man had fallen into the trap of trying to build himself up by tearing another down. What he said was simply untrue, but it caused me a great deal of pain.

Most pastors and Christian leaders want to do what is right. As we serve Christ and his church, we want to live above reproach. Yet despite our best efforts, people frequently misinterpret, although not always maliciously, our actions and words.

So I've found it isn't enough to be true to myself and God alone. I must go the second mile, not only that others might not be confused but that ministry might effectively continue. That was true when I was a pastor and it remains true in my role as president of a denomination. Here's how I try to do that.

Remember the Goal

First, I need realistic goals. The extra mile of pastoral integrity doesn't mean perfection, which is unachievable, but distinct progress in the Christian life. To paraphrase the apostle Paul, I have not fully attained it, but I am committed increasingly to follow Jesus as Lord, to walk in the Spirit.

As I walk in the Spirit, I stumble sometimes. All of us fail. That is not the question. The question is what we do with those sins and shortcomings. If we confess those sins to the Lord (enabled to do so by the power of the Holy Spirit) and if we deny ourselves, taking up the cross of Jesus daily, then we are sufficiently prepared to give spiritual leadership to others.

So I disagree with those who question a leader's integrity because of the leader's minor faults or infrequent misstatements. If integrity means perfection, then no one is eligible. And if true spirituality is judged on keeping the law, then as Paul shared with the Galatian church, Christ has died in vain.

Nonetheless, that is no excuse for mediocrity. God calls me as a leader to a higher standard, and with good reason. People use a leader's misconduct to justify themselves: "If he's pastor, and he does this, certainly it's right for me." Going the extra mile means walking with Christ so that others can follow me as I follow Christ.

That's why I abstain from drinking alcohol, for example. I don't pass judgment on Christians who with a clear conscience drink moderately. But I know even moderate drinking can invite problems, tensions, and temptations for many people. I am especially conscious of youth and their parents; I've counseled many alcoholic churched teens, and without exception, their parents were drinkers. If I were to become a stumbling block to even one person in this area, that to me would be one too many.

That's also why I try to handle family finances with integrity, honesty, and faithfulness. My wife, Jeannie, and I are committed to paying all our bills on time, even ahead of time. All through our married life, our credit has been A+.

And in the context of the office, I normally ask another, usually the church's business administrator, to hold me accountable for all paperwork, even beyond what is required by the auditor. I want to err on the side of safety in finances.

In a quiet, subtle way such financial practices become effective testimonies to others. To paraphrase the apostle Paul, if Christian leaders cannot handle their finances, how can they give effective leadership to the church?

Maintain Habits That Support Integrity

How we handle our finances is a matter of Christian stewardship. In the same way, God expects us to be good stewards of our time. That begins with our daily schedules. For me discipline and regularity are the keys. Few things sustain integrity like rhythmic work habits.

- *Devotions.* Rising early to seek the Lord — to spend time in the Scriptures and in prayer — is a basic discipline for most of us. And I'm careful to pursue personal devotions at this time, not turn it into sermon preparation. I do my devotions at home in my study, alternating them with exercise, jogging and walking, with my thoughts stayed on God, then returning to prayer and Scripture.

I've found that if I neglect this discipline, every other part of my day is compromised. Devotions insure a deeper, stronger walk with God. The deeper my walk with God, the better I'm able to resist temptation.

• *Study*. In the same way, I've found it best to reserve specific times for biblical study and sermon preparation. For years I've tried to set aside Monday, Tuesday, and Thursday mornings for study and sermon preparation. And I've found I can remain more focused when I study at home than at the church or office. I enjoy study and sermon preparation, but I'm not an intellectual. I find people more compelling than paper. At the church office, if someone came knocking with even a small emergency, it was nearly impossible for me to say no.

The discipline of secluded study helps me fulfill my responsibility to nourish and feed people through teaching and preaching. It prevents a sloppiness that would have disastrous long-term effects on the lives of the people God has entrusted to my care.

• *Family*. Integrity also requires that I schedule significant and appropriate times with my family. Frankly, most of us pastors won't spend significant time with our families if we do not schedule it in advance. So when I buy a new datebook, the first appointments I write into it are regular times with God and consistent times with my family.

Other disciplines have helped insure the quality of the time I spend at home. For example, I've found it best to keep administration at the office. At one church I fell into the trap of taking more and more administrative work home, compromising both family and study time. Several years ago, a light blinked on, and I decided, *No administration will be done at home.*

Another important discipline has been taking control of the home phone. How I did that varied with the size of the church and the setting. At one church I had a separate phone line for my home study. Only my family members, my secretary, and members of the pastoral team knew the number. Anytime I was there, I would answer; if I was out, the family let it ring.

Because a large church creates special visibility and problems, when I was at Lake Avenue I had an unlisted home number, which was nevertheless distributed freely within the church family. When I was studying and Jeannie wasn't home, an answering machine covered the family phone. In order to maintain quality interaction in my family, I felt I had to go the extra mile in these ways. It would not speak well for my integrity to have my family life fail while my pastorate succeeded.

• *Pastoral duties.* Because of the many demands on a pastor's time, I found it imperative to stick to a few practical disciplines while at the office.

For example, most of my Wednesdays were spent with the pastoral staff, both in business meetings and personal appointments. And once a month I had lunch with the chairpersons of the major boards as well as the church's chairman.

Then, within set boundaries, I tried to balance pastoring people with administrating the organization. Since administration and staff concerns always threatened to consume my time, I made it a special point to keep in touch with the people of the church. I've always had a policy of seeing anyone in the congregation who wanted to talk with me.

So I set aside a specific number of hours each week for counseling and personal contact with the congregation. Sometimes I would move around the church campus and see people in their daily settings. Sometimes I'd spend five minutes, sometimes fifty, doing this. It was important that I not seem too busy or important to be a pastor to my people.

But no matter how much I enjoy being with people, I've still had to balance the time I spend with people with study, administration, devotions, and family time. Ironically, people can disrupt that balance and all of our disciplines that sustain the integrity of our scheduling. The question is, how do we go the extra mile with them without going the extra five miles? Here's one way I found helpful.

Several years ago, a man young in the faith phoned several times to talk to me. Unfortunately he had the gift of calling when I was unavailable, and he began to get irate with my secretary, even screaming and swearing at her.

Finally I told my secretary, "Next time he calls, put him through, no matter whom I'm with; I've got to deal with this guy."

Once we connected, he was just as nice as could be. I told him, "I care about you, and we're going to help you, but I'm really sorry to hear how you've been treating my secretary." Then I arranged for him to come in for an appointment.

We sat down, and as I've done with many people, I explained to him carefully why it was impossible for me to see him every time he called. Then I said, "I'll make a deal with you. We'll set up two appointments a year together. At other times, if you need help, we always have a pastor on call, twenty-four hours a day, every day."

It worked great. We would talk for an hour, sipping soft drinks. I liked spending time with him, and he felt special.

Good habits — with God, with family, with the church — help me maintain my integrity because they help me stay on track in all my responsibilities.

Be in the World but a Cut Above It

Several years ago I prayed the invocation at a major community dinner, a fund-raising event for a hospital. The Los Angeles chief of police was speaker, and during the dinner I was seated next to him. The servers began pouring wine. In such situations, though I don't drink, I often allow them to fill the glass so they won't keep asking. That particular evening I said, "No, thank you," and requested they take the glass.

The next morning on the front page of the daily newspaper appeared a picture of the chief of police with me sitting by his side, his wine glass in front of him, mine gone. My first thought was how it would have appeared to some if I had allowed the waiter to leave a filled glass.

That experience, among many others, brought home to me the truth that when I'm on secular turf, my integrity is examined even more closely. So going the extra mile is even more important when I find myself in a public setting. For me this means two things.

• *Take care in potentially compromising situations.* For instance, when I take my secretary to lunch, Jeannie, my wife, always goes with us. Although in this age it's normal for businessmen and businesswomen to lunch together, in my role many could misinterpret my conduct.

To take another example, though I didn't particularly like the environment, as a pastor I often would attend cocktail parties at the Rotary Club. I found it a significant time to build relationships and carry on an effective ministry; in such settings unbelievers drop defenses and talk more openly.

Yet to be above reproach, I would begin the evening by getting a Coke in hand. Then I found it easier to visit freely without continually having to turn down offers of alcoholic beverages from servers. In such situations I don't want to appear "holier than thou," but I do want to be above reproach.

• *Avoid certain activities altogether.* I believe there are certain activities that Christian leaders simply cannot attend with integrity. I am not suggesting we establish legalistic standards, but I have seen many pastors and Christian leaders become involved in activities that are detrimental to them, their families, and the people they serve.

Take, for example, the area of entertainment, one of the greatest challenges for Christians in our society. I have announced publicly to my congregations that I wouldn't attend R-rated movies. For that matter, there are many PG and PG-13 movies I will not attend. As a Christian leader, it's one way I can model for others a distinctively Christian lifestyle.

As the Gallup poll reflects, there seems to be little difference in lifestyle or morality between those who have made a commitment to Jesus Christ and those who have not. That is tragic. The life of authentic Christian discipleship should be distinctively different. Jesus Christ holds us to a life of personal purity and holiness. Scripture tells us to flee lust and sexual immorality. And I recognize that our spiritual sensitivities can be subtly but profoundly affected by what we read, see, and experience.

I'm especially concerned about Christian young people, who, surrounded by unbelieving peers who guzzle pop entertainment bilge water, are growing up with lax standards. Teenagers often can't understand why a well-meaning Christian adult distinguishes between one PG movie and another, between one R-rated movie and another. Lacking such discernment, kids are approving of things we never would.

Although I may miss some films with redeeming value, I've made this commitment for the sake of extra-mile pastoral integrity.

Handle Gifts and Honoraria with Care

In many secular organizations, an employee is expected to turn over to his employer any honoraria earned while on the job. Pastors, however, have traditionally accepted honoraria for weddings, funerals, and guest speaking. Some suggest that in this case, the world has loftier standards, and they question pastors' integrity in taking honoraria.

However, there is a clear historical rationale for pastors doing so. Pastors have always been paid differently than have other vocations in our society. In the past, because clergy salaries were often modest, churches frequently supplemented pastors' income by providing a parsonage. In addition, rural churches gave pastors vegetables, meat, and other food that came from their farms. It was within this context that ministers were paid honoraria at special functions such as weddings and funerals.

So given this historical context, it is certainly legitimate for churches to provide such honoraria. I have known pastors who have used honoraria for book accounts. I have one pastor friend who uses his honoraria for his family vacation.

Still, some ministers are not comfortable receiving honoraria. For example, my father, a Presbyterian minister in rural America, felt that weddings and funerals were merely an extension of his pastoral ministry. He rarely, if ever, accepted honoraria.

Although I don't think refusing honoraria is a necessity, to go the extra mile of integrity, I have imitated my dad. But for all pastors, integrity requires that we follow the policy of our given church or ministry.

For example, when I was with the Billy Graham Association, all outside honoraria, by company policy, went to the association. So it depends on the compensation package as well as the church's expectations and guidelines.

Personal gifts to the pastor or church leader also become integrity issues. Some people give gifts as a way of gaining leverage over the pastor and the church. Accepting gifts can unconsciously imply favoritism and affect how we preach the Word. The larger the gift, the more of an issue it becomes.

Even with these guidelines and doing all we can to live above reproach, I have found that pastors cannot control how others perceive their integrity quotient. People often project their own weaknesses on leaders. Frequently this is a painful experience for us. Fortunately, at other times the situation can be humorous.

For example, several years ago, a woman sent me a letter that read something like this: "Dear Dr. Cedar: I've never met you personally, but I've heard you preach, and I think I can recognize you. I was in a restaurant recently when a man walked in who looked like you. I wasn't sure, so I thought I'd wait until the meal was served and, if you prayed, then I would know it was probably you."

Then the whole tone of the letter changed: "You didn't pray!" For the rest of the letter she assaulted me for not praying in public. She signed her name but gave no address or phone number. I was both upset and amused. Not only had I never been in that restaurant, I had never even heard of it!

Still, I have found that going the extra mile more often than not has enhanced not only the effectiveness of my ministry but also my life. I consider it a privilege to try to live above reproach. In fact, I believe God created us to live so, and I'm convinced that it is the most fulfilling kind of lifestyle.

Furthermore, I've found the best way for me to determine

how I live is to aim to live as Jesus would live. The best questions we can ask ourselves are: *What would Jesus do in this situation? What would Jesus say? How would Jesus respond?*

In short, if we are to serve our Lord Jesus Christ and lead his people, we need to follow him as Lord. As the old hymn suggests, we need to "let the beauty of Jesus be seen" in us.

Only God knows the score, so I should not weigh too heavily or take too seriously what I or anybody else thinks of me. But since he will one day ask me the Big Faithfulness Question, I'd better ask myself a few like it until that day.

— Ben Patterson

CHAPTER ELEVEN

How Do I Evaluate Myself?

How do I evaluate myself? First I'll give you the short answer, then the long.

The short answer is I don't, or rather I can't or shouldn't. If I read the New Testament correctly, to do so may border on the presumptuous. The apostle Paul counseled a pious, even belligerent agnosticism regarding self-evaluation: "I care very little if I am judged by you or by any human court; indeed, I do not even judge myself. My conscience is clear, but that does not make me innocent. It is the Lord who judges me." So much for self-evaluation or any human evaluation. God is the judge, not us — case closed, end of discussion, end of chapter, and end of the personnel committee of my church.

The long answer starts with the short answer and then proceeds delicately to reopen the discussion and perhaps reestablish the personnel committee by asking some hard questions about faithfulness. Paul said that because he understood himself to be a steward of the gospel. A steward is someone who has been entrusted with another person's property and charged with managing it in the owner's interests. Faithfulness is the measure of the steward, says Paul: "Now it is required that those who have been given a trust must prove faithful."

All that matters to him is that he be able to answer yes to the question he knows he and every human being will one day be asked by God: "Did you do what I wanted with what I gave you, the way I wanted you to?" In other words, "Were you faithful?"

So how do I evaluate myself? I start by recognizing, up front, that only God knows the score and that I should not weigh too heavily or take too seriously what I or anybody else thinks of me. But since he will one day ask me the Big Faithfulness Question, I'd better ask myself a few like it until that day. But always with the Big Qualifier hanging over the exercise, proceeding cautiously, humbly.

How Impressed Am I with "Success"?

Numbers are notoriously unreliable measures of success. You know that; I know that. The "bigger is better" credo has been so thoroughly discredited that no one gives it any attention anymore.

So why does my shirt collar start unaccountably to tighten around my neck when I read that church attendance is down this year compared to last? Why do we keep records anyway? And continually we make projections, projections, projections. There's more of the ecclesiastical actuary in me than I'd like to admit.

But when I look at the valuation the risen Christ gives to the seven churches in Asia Minor, a totally different scale of measurement emerges. The richest, in Laodicea, is really the poorest. The busiest, in Ephesus, is chided for its lovelessness. The only churches that receive unqualified commendation from the Lord are Smyrna and Philadelphia, congregations he describes as afflicted, poor, and weak. Once again, it is as he said it would be: the first are last and the last are first.

Clarence Jordan had a dream to build a Christian community in the deep South, a community that would model reconciliation between the races. So he brought black and white together to work and worship at Koinonia Farm, near Americus, Georgia. For a while they suffered bravely through the predictable threats and beatings from the neighboring townspeople. And when the farm was burned down, the whole project seemed to have disintegrated. Newspaper reporters came out to ask Jordan some painful questions, the most bitter being, "Well, Clarence, just how successful do you think this whole thing has been?" Jordan thought for a moment and answered softly, "About as successful as the cross."

If big numbers are a sign of lots of new people discovering a vital faith at the church I pastor, then I will rejoice. If a growing budget is a sign of a deepening sense of Christian stewardship among my people, then I will be thankful and glad. But there is no way for me to know conclusively that those two signs of institutional success have anything to do with success in the kingdom of God. Indeed, the struggling pastor with dwindling numbers may be achieving a spectacular kingdom success by simply hanging on and faithfully doing the best he knows how, even if his best isn't very good.

The degree to which I find myself dazzled by my institutional successes may be a sign of deep failure spiritually, an indicator that I have forgotten that faithfulness, not "success," is what delights the Lord, that after urging everyone else to run the race, I myself have been disqualified.

Do I Love the People I Serve?

Not to love those whom I serve would be a contradiction in terms, a desperate betrayal of what Jesus said was the essence of authentic service: to lay down my life for my brothers and sisters. In 1 Corinthians 13 Paul says it is possible to be eloquent, wise, generous, sacrificial, and even spiritual — in short to be all the things most churches would like their pastors to be — and amount to absolutely nothing. For without love that is what all these ingredients for institutional success ultimately amount to.

It is possible to cut quite a fine figure as a preacher and not love those to whom I preach, to receive human praise and salary increases and not love those who praise me and pay me, to be used of God to win souls and heal the sick and nevertheless fail at love. Even when I am at my best, my success in any of these areas is no more than the result of God's sovereign choice to use me in spite of, not because of who I am. After all, if he did it with Balaam's ass, he can do it with me. And he has.

Do I love them? It's hard to know. Sometimes they may feel I do when I don't and feel I don't when I do. They may mistake my introversion for coldness and the strength of my bear hugs for warmth. Only God knows. But I believe there are some clues:

• *Preaching.* If I find it too easy to be the prophet, to speak God's hard word to them, then I probably don't love them enough. If with St. Paul, my warnings come with tears, I probably do. Harsh words, if they must be spoken, should always be costly.

• *My expectations.* If my affection for my people is both patient and relentless, I probably love them. If it is only patient or only relentless, either I probably don't love them, or it means my love is seriously flawed. George MacDonald said God is easy to please but impossible to satisfy, meaning good Father that he is, he is delighted at our every effort to grow (his love is patient) but will never rest until his children have grown to their full stature in Christ (his love is relentless).

Neither permissiveness nor perfectionism will do; acceptance and challenge, unconditional love and demand must stand side by side. I must love my people as they are, and love them enough not to let them stay where they are.

• *Their expectations.* We all know how we'd like others to love us, but sometimes they may have another idea. Sometimes people's expectations will be in conflict with mine. My idea of relentless love may be received as quite the opposite, as no love at all.

For example, I believe that a hospital call by a layperson gifted by the Holy Spirit is every bit as "valid" as a hospital call by an ordained clergyperson, namely me, who may not be gifted to that sort of thing. Does it mean I don't love my congregation if I don't make many hospital calls? No way. In fact, if I delegate such ministry to laypeople it may be an act of love, because it helps my people see the truth of the priesthood of all believers.

Of course, it isn't all a matter of me lovingly violating their expectations. It can work the other way, and if I love my people I will listen thoughtfully and compassionately to what they want from me. I will change my agenda for ministry accordingly if the Holy Spirit confirms in my own heart what they tell me they need.

For the most part, however, I would rather be a general than a mayor. My call to ministry is weighted decidedly on the side of visionary, directive leadership. I do need to listen to my people but more to give me a sense of *how* to get where we should go than to find out *where* we should go. I need to be nurtured in aloneness with God and with men and women, hopefully elders and staff, who have a similar bent. Perhaps it's arrogance, but I'm convinced that the church is in dire need of people like that — leaders who will shape the church more than it shapes them. That is the unique kind of love a pastor must give the church.

• *Prayer*. If intercession is infrequent and perfunctory, I probably don't love my people. If standing before God on their behalf is at the heart of what I do for them, I probably do. The apostle Paul was impressed with what he termed the "hard work" a certain pastor named Epaphras was doing for his people. He even wrote to tell them so. It is remarkable that his tribute was given to a man who was not at home with his people, but with Paul. His "hard work" was being accomplished in absentia, "wrestling in prayer" on their behalf, miles away physically but right by their side spiritually.

The opposite can be true — and often is: I can be right by my people's side physically but miles away spiritually if I do not hold them up before God in prayer continually.

To get an idea of how prayer is a solid act of love, search Paul's epistles. You will discover not only his lovely prayers for his people — models of pastoral love — but that the request he most often makes is that they pray for him too. He will be deeply grateful for their money and for their visits but will rarely ask for these. Presumably he believes that if people pray for him, the rest will follow.

I have heard far too many cutesy little sermon illustrations contrasting the so-called practical "doer" with the so-called impractical "pray-er." You've probably heard them too: on the one hand there is the practical man who knows when to get off his knees and do something for others. On the other hand there is the mystic who dreams of pie-in-the-sky on his knees when he should be on his feet rolling the dough for the crust. I have yet to meet this straw man.

• *Ends and means.* A long time ago, I watched bewildered as one stalwart church worker after another fell prey to that nebulous thing we call "burnout." So many good things seemed to be happening in the church: growth everywhere, new people, new programs, more of this, better of that.

The problem was we were making stupendous advances in the growth of the institution on the backs of the people making the advances possible. We were achieving what appeared to be Christian ends with non-Christian means.

But in the Kingdom of God the means and the ends must be in harmony. No end justifies a means that destroys people. If church growth is bought at the price of a broken marriage or broken health or broken faith, then only the church grew while the Kingdom retreated.

My ministry is for the sake of Christ and those for whom he died. If either is slighted, what I'm doing ceases to be ministry. That includes what happens in my own marriage and family.

What Do My Godly and Wise Peers Think?

One day Piglet came upon dear, dense Winnie-the-Pooh in the snowy woods, who was totally absorbed in tracking a strange animal. Joining him, Piglet too scrutinized the tracks and squeaked with excitement, "Oh, Pooh! Do you think it's a . . . a . . . a Woozle?"

"It may be," said Pooh, and off they went in pursuit of this dreaded beast. A little later they noticed the tracks of another animal traveling with the Woozle. Then after a while the tracks of a third and a fourth. The dread of what they might discover became too much for Piglet who lamely excused himself from the adventure.

Pooh persisted in the hunt until Christopher Robin came along. "Silly old Bear," said Robin, "what were you doing?" He then pointed out that Pooh and Piglet had been walking in circles around the grove. Pooh blushed as he gingerly extended a paw toward one of the Woozle tracks. It was just as he feared: he had been tracking himself.

Self-evaluation can be a lot like tracking a Woozle: just a solipsistic exercise in navel gazing, especially for people like me who tend toward strong, individualistic leadership stances. I need some kind of outside perspective, some objective input as to how I'm doing.

A covenant or support group of peers can do this. Invaluable was the pastors' covenant group I was a part of for twelve years before I moved to a new pastorate. They were a godly and wise bunch of brothers who were able to give me a perspective on myself that I simply could never have acquired on my own. They loved me; they loved the church of Christ; they understood its special workings and challenges. And they were not embroiled in my particular set of circumstances. In other words, they were suited as few can be to give me an objective look at myself and my ministry.

Early in my ministry I was told by a wise and good humored veteran of ecclesiastical wars to weigh my criticism, not count it. I weigh heavily the criticism that comes from men like these. I am finding such a group in my new situation.

Does My Work Point Away from Me to God?

Success in the ministry breeds praise. And it sure feels good once in a while, doesn't it? There is nothing wrong with this, and I think it is a special grace for a pastor to be able to warmly and humbly receive applause.

Over the years of my ministry, from time to time God has mercifully sent me a Barnabas, a "son of encouragement," at the times I most needed to be reminded that my work was not in vain. Certainly it is a good thing for a grateful congregation to express its love and gratitude for the hard work we do.

We should receive the kudos but hold them lightly, for all success comes from God. We earthenware pots have the inestimable privilege of holding in ourselves the treasure of the Gospel, so that it will be obvious to all who see that the treasure is God, not us.

Am I content for this to be so? Am I satisfied to be mere earthenware? Or do I wish I were bone china or to be thought of as such? Does my ministry point away from me to the Lord? After I preach a great sermon, do my people walk away aware of how great God is or of how well I said he is great? My success or failure in the work of the kingdom hinges on how that question is answered.

Have I Taken the Long View?

That's my final question for self-evaluation. Am I quick to remember that, as Paul put it, we should "judge nothing before its time"? No amount of praise and recognition and church growth is sufficient for me to make a final judgment on the success of my ministry. The final judgment comes only at the Final Judgment.

So I must relax and keep working until the end. The ministry is like farming: there is cultivation and planting and fertilizing and watering, and then waiting for the harvest. The proof of the crop is in the crop and not a moment sooner.

So what do I do as I wait? I do everything I know to honor God. I pray for greater love and wisdom, and lacking them, I sometimes sin boldly and cry out for God's mercy. And I long to one day hear him say to me, "Well done, good and faithful servant."

To have a pastor's heart means to enter into the joy as well as the pain of our congregations, even when the joy and the pain are just moments apart.

— Kent Hughes

Maintaining a Pastor's Heart

Kirsten is blond and blue-eyed, a stunning beauty. She has attended our church for several years and has been a deeply committed Christian for as long as I've known her. When she became engaged to a young man named Stephen, the two of them asked me to do their wedding.

Together, they were a picture-perfect couple. Kirsten's tall athletic beauty was matched by Stephen's lean, muscular good looks. Though only in his mid-twenties, Stephen was already employed in an extremely lucrative profession. In addition, Stephen had recently committed his life to the Lord and had immediately immersed himself in his newfound faith.

The day of the wedding came — a rainy day in spring. Yet nothing, not even rain, could dampen the joy and excitement of that day — or so I thought.

The wedding was scheduled for 4:30 in the afternoon. I was already at church at 3:30, preparing for the wedding ceremony, when the phone rang. It was Janet, a young woman in our congregation. Her husband Ray, who was only in his late thirties, had died suddenly only an hour before. He had no history of heart problems, yet he had dropped dead of a massive heart attack while doing light yard work.

Compressed into the space of a couple hours on this rainy spring was the full range of emotions that sometimes ebb, sometimes surge in the heart of a pastor. Here were the great joys, the rude shocks, the deep sorrows, all jumbled together. Ray was one of the most vital members of my congregation. In a heartbeat, he was gone. How do you go into the sanctuary and perform a wedding ceremony on top of news like that?

And yet doing just that is what is required of a pastor. We enter into the joy as well as the pain of our congregation, even when the joy and the pain are just moments apart. To be a pastor is to immerse ourselves authentically in the emotion of the moment, whatever that moment means in the life of our congregation.

So I performed the wedding ceremony. It was a joyous wedding, and I fully entered into that joy, sharing in the triumph of my friends Stephen and Kirsten.

Then, as soon as the wedding was over, I got in my car, drove home through the rain, picked up my wife Barbara, and went to comfort the grieving young widow. For her, it was a time of intense grief, and my wife and I entered into that aching grief along with her and her family and friends.

It is rare, of course, for the highs and lows to come as crowded together as they did that day. But I look back on the whipsawing emotions of that afternoon as an "emotional electrocardiogram" — a tracing of a few heartbeats that symbolize the entire sweep of a pastor's life and ministry.

Good Pastors Have Heart Problems

To have a pastor's heart, it is necessary to have a heart problem — an enlarged heart. To be effective pastors, we must enlarge our love and make ourselves vulnerable. And when we do that, it is inevitable that we will experience a godly angina, a deep and piercing pain of the heart. As C. S. Lewis observes in *The Four Loves*, a heart that loves is a heart that knows pain:

> To love at all is to be vulnerable. Love anything, and your heart will certainly be wrung and possibly be broken. If you want to be sure of keeping it intact, you must give your heart to no one, not even to an animal. Wrap it carefully round with hobbies and little luxuries; avoid all entanglements; lock it up safe in the casket or coffin of your selfishness. But in that casket — safe, dark, motionless, airless — it will change. It will not be broken; it will become unbreakable, impenetrable, irredeemable. The alternative to tragedy, or at least the risk of tragedy, is damnation. The only place outside Heaven where you can be perfectly safe from all the dangers and perturbations of love is Hell.

One man who had an enlarged pastor's heart was an English missionary named James Gilmour. Beginning in the 1870s, he was the pioneering missionary to Mongolia, scattering the gospel over completely unplowed ground. Upon his arrival in Mongolia, he wrote in his journal, "Several huts in sight! When shall I be able to speak to the people? O Lord, suggest by the Spirit how I should come among them, and guide me in gaining the language, and in preparing myself to teach the life and love of Christ Jesus!"

Twenty years later, his missionary effort in Mongolia came to a close, and he made a final entry in his journal, which read, "In the shape of converts I have seen no result. I have not, as far as I am aware, seen anyone who even wanted to be a Christian." Almost a quarter century of labor and not a single convert!

How could a man give that much of his life to a missionary effort without ever seeing any results from his labor? What could have compelled him to stay, year after year, in the face of such complete rejection? Only one thing: an enlarged heart, a vulnerable heart, and ultimately a broken heart, full of pastoral love and concern for people.

A variety of people and circumstances common to the pastorate make maintaining a pastor's heart a challenge. But a few observations and strategies have been of great help to me.

Developing a Heart for the Unlovely

There are times when we are called to counsel people who are so ego centered and inward — *imploded* — that it takes everything we have to listen to them. I have actually found myself unconsciously digging my nails into my palms to maintain concentration when listening to such people, for there are few things more tedious than the soliloquy of a self-centered soul.

So how do we in ministry maintain a pastor's heart for such people? By acting as if we love them, by "putting on love." We listen to the monologue, offer counsel, confront, and pray as a volitional act of love. And in doing so we actually do love and develop love.

This was a family friend's poignant experience when she and her husband spent a missionary furlough here in the States. As would be expected, she was looking forward to a time of rest and quiet — especially since she was going to have a place of her own, for they had been able to buy a small townhouse with their meager resources. She is creative and, with little, made her townhouse quite attractive, especially her patio.

All went well until new neighbors, who could be best described as "coarse," moved in. They played loud music day and night, overlaid with constant shouts and obscenities. Soon their windows were broken and unrepaired. They urinated on the front yard in broad daylight. Not only were they degenerate, they also seemed mentally deficient — beyond help. My friend could see no good in them whatsoever.

During all this she had been praying that the Lord would make her more loving, but all she could muster was disgust and rejection. Then came the day when she returned home to find that her neighbor's children had scaled her patio wall, discovered a can of orange paint, and sprayed her patio — walls, floors, everything.

She tried to pray but found herself crying and saying, "I hate them! I don't have it in myself to love. I hate them!"

She knew her heart was in trouble and began to converse with the Lord in her inner being, and God's Word came to her from Colossians, "And beyond all these things put on love, which is the perfect bond of unity " (3:14). *How do I put on love?* she wondered, *It seems so impossible and hypocritical.*

Finally, she concluded that putting on love must, in some way, be like putting on a coat. And so, phony or not, this is what she determined to do. She willfully cloaked herself in the love of God. She began by making a list of what she would do if she really loved them: bake cookies, offer to baby-sit free, invite the mother over for coffee. Soon she found herself, pie in hand, knocking on the door.

In the following weeks, she carried out her love list. And gradually she began to understand something of the pressures in their lives. And she began to truly care.

The day came that the family had to move. And do you know what happened? Our friend wept! She had seen no change in them, but she had changed. By putting on love she had come to love.

So it will be for the pastor who, in obedience to God's Word, puts on love for the unlovely. Hypocrisy? No. Obedience to God's Word is the path to authenticity — and a loving pastor's heart.

Mercy for the Manipulative

Mrs. Crawford was an attractive woman in her forties who had recently been through a divorce. At the time she came to me for counseling, she was a lonely and troubled woman — and also manipulative. As I listened to her during her second appointment, I was taken back by her unexpectedly saying, "I am so lonely. And you're so cold and distant."

Clearly she was trying to make me feel responsible for her loneliness, while at the same time attacking my pastoral persona — the idea being that if I were a good pastor, I would come around the table and be less "distant."

Without a moment's pause I looked Mrs. Crawford in the eyes

and said with a consciously arctic tone, "There's a table here between you and me. That table is here for a reason. And you know what it is. You have probably noticed that I have left the door ajar. This is because I care for you and my ministry. Now, if I was as cold and aloof as you say I am, I wouldn't be sitting here trying to help you."

That was the end of the manipulation! And we proceeded to deal with her concerns. I counseled her one more time — giving her substantial help, I think, and then referred her to a competent Christian woman in our church, under whose guidance she did well.

A pastor's heart, though tender and compassionate, must never be naive or easily intimidated. A heart that can be manipulated will help no one. As I like to say, "I may be born again, but I wasn't born yesterday!"

Care-full Administration

Many pastors loathe administration because they don't enjoy it and because they regard administrative duties as keeping them from "ministry" — prayer, the study of God's Word, and shepherding the flock. Some are convinced that administration is detrimental to a pastor's heart.

And, indeed, administration can squeeze out the essentials. Not a few have been suffocated by the endless letters, memos, newsletters, and phone calls, as well as staff, board, committee, and private meetings.

I manage to carve out a healthy twenty-five to thirty hours a week for prayer, study, and sermon preparation. Sometimes I'd still like to set fire to the memos and notes to call people back that sit on my desk. Yet I refuse to abandon administration because I've come to see how it can enhance my essential ministry — caring for the church.

The Greek word for *administration* literally refers to a helmsman or a captain who steers a boat. In the New Testament, then, it carries the meaning "one who guides or governs." To put it another way, administration is a way to disciple people, to guide people into a greater experience of God's love and a fuller obedience to his commands.

Administrating a multiple staff is time consuming to say the least. In addition to a weekly four-hour breakfast, prayer, and staff meeting, I usually consult individually with each staff member through the week. During these meetings my philosophy and vision are most effectively communicated — that's when they are "caught." And through the staff, I'm giving pastoral direction to the entire church.

This is also true of the prosaic "busy things" that try to crowd our lives — the letters, memos, and phone calls. However, I've noticed that the tone of letters and conversations, over time, have a vast influence over the ethos and direction of a church.

Similarly, I've found that the time I've invested in meetings with our Council of Elders (the ruling board of our church) has paid rich pastoral dividends. We've not only developed close relationships, they've also become strong advocates of the church's ministry. My pastoral heart has been multiplied by administration.

When I view administration not as "grunt work" but as work that advances the larger goals of glorifying our Lord and equipping and sanctifying his people, then these tasks cease to be onerous. No longer do I resist the "intrusion" of these chores on my ministry, because they are indispensable to effective ministry. Ultimately, the distinction between what is "administration" and what is "ministerial" is simply a matter of perspective. For me administration is a matter of the heart — a form of pastoral care.

Choreographing Compassion

I sometimes hear pastors moan that it's almost impossible to maintain a pastor's heart under the pressure of a jam-packed, morning-to-midnight schedule. And I think it's true: the kind of pressure-cooker existence many pastors endure can indeed squeeze the heart right out of a person. There have certainly been times in my own ministry when I have felt that way.

Yet at such times, I have to ask myself, *Who packed your schedule, Kent?* And then I have to confess before God, "I packed it. I didn't say no to this event. I agreed to write that article. I took on that extra speaking engagement."

I am responsible for the disordered state of my schedule —not my parishioners, not my elders, not my secretary. If other people seem to be controlling my time, it's because I have abdicated, handed control over to them. I have no one to blame but myself.

Amazingly, we seem to find the time to do those things we truly want to do. If we like to garden, we find time to get out in the yard and putter. If we like baseball or football, we manage to get in a game or two during the week, even if other things have to take a back seat.

I believe most of us have all the time we need to do what really needs to get done. The problem is that we shoot ourselves in the wristwatch by failing to adequately choreograph our schedules. The axiom: If we do not control our time, someone else will.

For me, this means I must lay out my schedule to my secretary. I say, "I have time for appointments between 3:00 and 5:00 P.M. on these days. I have lunch appointments open on these days. If there are some who can't see me during those hours because of their jobs, I can take appointments from 8:30 to 10:00 on Wednesday nights, or Thursday morning for early breakfast." And I don't vary those boundaries, except, of course, in the case of a genuine emergency — and there are many!

Appointments are set up in blocks of a half hour, no more. Most people, if they know they have thirty minutes, get down to what they want to talk about. If more time is needed, we can schedule an additional appointment. That may sound rigid. But I find I'm more effective in caring for the deep human needs of my congregation by being in control of my time. I have been able to put my pastor's heart to more effective use.

Threats to a Pastor's Heart

If some areas of the pastorate challenge our ability to maintain a pastor's heart, other things threaten to undermine it completely.

● *Our emotional neediness.* Our pastor's heart can easily be undermined by our own emotional neediness. Many of us can put our finger right on the emotional or spiritual problems of our parishioners, while being completely ignorant of the hidden needs, urges, and drives that propel our own lives.

Some of us are literally need driven. We need to be needed. We derive our feelings of self-worth and success as a pastor from having people affirm us, depend on us, crowd our schedule, and tell us how wonderfully self-sacrificing we are. So we run around, answering the phones, going to all the meetings, working around the clock — all because of our feelings of personal inadequacy, our craving to be liked by others, our need to be needed.

To maintain a genuine pastor's heart in the face of this temptation, I've found it helpful to remind myself of the obvious: I am not God. I am not responsible to answer to everyone's needs. Furthermore, God doesn't need me, nor does the church. I am, in fact, expendable. God can replace me at the drop of a hat.

Once this truth sinks in, I've found I can do my job more effectively and more intelligently. I learn to delegate more, to choreograph my schedule more sensibly, and to live realistically within my limits.

• *Criticism.* A pastor's heart can also be undermined by criticism and opposition. Unfortunately, criticism just goes with the pastoral turf. We can't escape it.

To begin with, all pastors are human and make mistakes, so a lot of criticism we receive is accurate, whether or not it is well-intentioned. Criticism always stings. However, it is indispensable to our learning and growth.

But apart from the constructive criticism that comes our way, there also come unjust attacks in the form of rumors, innuendoes about our character, and insults — sometimes blatant and sometimes subtle. The criticisms we take home are the ones that can erode a pastor's heart.

Moreover, pastors rarely suffer unfair criticism alone. Spouses sometimes suffer these injustices even more intensely than pastors. A typical example is for a husband to come home and share some barb he has received that day, and then forget it — only to find days later that his wife is still smarting!

What to do when we're attacked? Certainly criticism must be met with a gentle spirit and forgiveness. As Frederick Buechner has reminded us, we must resist the temptation to lick our wounds and chew on our grievances because we will find that the skeleton at the front is us!

Yet at the same time, many pastors by temperament and training wrongly absorb abuse — and thus allow harm to come to the people they love the most.

But being an ecclesiastical doormat is not biblical. Sometimes for the sake of the church, my family, and the critical offender, I must confront my critic. Pastors' hearts can be undermined by criticism if they turn us into passive pastoral punching bags, hemorrhaging unseen anger and bitterness till our insides are empty.

My answer is not to start swinging. There are times, for which the Scripture supplies guidance (Matthew 18:15–17, Galatians 6:1), to confront destructive critics.

But in any case, I've found it most helpful to follow the model given by Jesus. When he was reviled, he reviled not. He never sought redress. He forgave his enemies. Moreover, he prayed for those who hurt him. In fact, I regularly pray for my critics, asking God to bless them.

Job tells us that "the Lord restored the fortunes of Job" when Job prayed for his detractors (Job 42:10). My experience reveals that in terms of my external relationships with my critics, sometimes that happens and sometimes not. But when I follow the example of Jesus, my pastoral heart is restored — and strengthened.

● *Problems at home.* There have been times when listening to a parishioner intone a prosaic concern that I have thought, *I'll trade you for some of mine!*

Concern over one of my children or a spat with my wife can loom bigger than life, emptying me of my ability to concentrate and give the needed empathy, intelligent interaction, and spiritual council my people so need.

The irony is that giving my people the honest, heart-felt attention and engagement they need is precisely the thing that can bring toxic stresses to the manse.

A pastor friend was sitting at the breakfast table one morning with his family. His children were trying to talk to him, but his mind was already at church, contemplating the problems of his people. Finally, his exasperated teenage daughter confronted him.

"Dad," she said, "we don't mind you being gone all the time, but when you're here, we want you to be *here*."

His daughter was right. We cannot allow the church to dominate our mealtimes, family times, vacation times, and days off. When I am with those closest to me, I want to give them, if anything, closer attention than I give my congregation.

This brings me back to my belief that I should wade fully into the emotional current of whatever situation I find myself in, as difficult as that might be. In the long run, that's a better plan than shutting off one part of my life to emotions, or worse, confusing people by bringing the emotions of one setting into another.

Sometimes, in the course of my work as a pastor, depressing or infuriating things happen. But my children don't need to have a depressed or angry father at the dinner table. They need a father who is willing to give them as much attention and care as he gives all those people who stream through his office every day.

I have always tried to remember that my children's whole world is as big as my world. So I try to ask them, "How did your day go? What did you learn? Did you have any problems today?" And then I need to genuinely listen and make eye contact with them when they talk.

So, I try not to take the family's dirty laundry to church with me, nor the church's dirty laundry to my home.

Phillips Brooks, the Episcopal bishop of Boston in the late 1800's, as well as the author of the hymn "O Little Town of Bethlehem," made a statement in one of his Yale lectures on preaching that has always challenged me:

> *To be a true minister to men is always to accept new happiness and new distress. . . . The man who gives himself to other men can never*

be a wholly sad man, but no more can he be a man of unclouded gladness. To him shall come with every deeper consecration a before untasted joy, but in the same cup shall be mixed a sorrow that was beyond his power to feel before.

In some ways, we have the toughest, most heartbreaking, most frustrating, yet most rewarding job in the world. We get up every morning knowing the job will never be finished in our lifetime yet willing to go through it again and again — preaching the Word, shoving the papers from one basket to the other, holding the hands of the sick and the dying, rejoicing with those who rejoice, weeping with those who weep.

We do it, of course, because deep within us there beats an enlarged heart, pierced with holy joy and holy pain, a heart that yearns to beat in sync with the heart of the Good Shepherd himself.

Pastoring is not something ministers so much ponder;
pastor *is something they* are.

Mark Galli

Epilogue

An unexamined life, Socrates told us, is not worth living. And an unexamined minister's life is probably, well, a mess. Pastors often find themselves in the midst of too many wanting too much too soon. These authors have tried to help pastors step away momentarily from the ecclesiastical confusion and breathe and think and reorder their life work.

Yet if an unexamined life is not worth living, an overexamined life is weariness to the flesh. As much as these three men have given serious attention to the pastoral role, they've not spent a lot of time brooding about it. When we would ask them about the pastoral role, it was as if they had to jog their memories to bring the issue to consciousness.

To put it another way, they are like most pastors: they simply live out the pastoral role. Pastors are first and foremost human beings committed to Christ. Yet in some sense, pastoring is an extension of their being. It's not something they ponder; *pastor* is something they are.

Pastors are like eagles. Eagles, like other birds, have feathers and beaks and claws. Then again, birds fly; eagles soar. Eagles are a special order of bird, and when they act like what they are, they are a magnificent bird.

At times, pastors will stop to reflect on their role: *When and where am I father, mother, parent, community activist, preacher, administrator? When am I just a person?* But most of the time, they don't think and worry and ponder about the when and how and what. When they're at their best, they simply soar, living out the magnificent call God has given them.